THE ODD ONE IN

SHORT CIRCUITS
Slavoj Žižek, editor

The Puppet and the Dwarf: The Perverse Core of Christianity, by Slavoj Žižek

The Shortest Shadow: Nietzsche's Philosophy of the Two, by Alenka Zupančič

Is Oedipus Online? Siting Freud after Freud, by Jerry Aline Flieger

Interrogation Machine: Laibach and NSK, by Alexei Monroe

The Parallax View, by Slavoj Žižek

A Voice and Nothing More, by Mladen Dolar

Subjectivity and Otherness: A Philosophical Reading of Lacan, by Lorenzo Chiesa

The Odd One In: On Comedy, by Alenka Zupančič

THE ODD ONE IN

On Comedy

Alenka Zupančič

THE MIT PRESS   CAMBRIDGE, MASSACHUSETTS   LONDON, ENGLAND

This book was set in Joanna and Copperplate 33bc by Graphic Composition, Inc., Athens, Georgia.

Library of Congress Cataloging-in-Publication Data

Zupančič, Alenka.
     The odd one in : on comedy / Alenka Zupančič.
          p. cm. — (Short circuits)
     Includes bibliographical references.
     ISBN 978-0-262-74031-9 (pbk. : alk. paper)
     1. Comic, The. 2. Comedy. I. Title.
BH301.C7Z87 2007
700'.417—dc22
                                                          2007018868

To Martin

CONTENTS

A short circuit occurs when there is a faulty connection in the network—faulty, of course, from the standpoint of the network's smooth functioning. Is not the shock of short-circuiting, therefore, one of the best metaphors for a critical reading? Is not one of the most effective critical procedures to cross wires that don't usually touch: to take a major classic (text, author, notion) and read it in a short-circuiting way, through the lens of a "minor" author, text, or conceptual apparatus ("minor" should be understood here in Deleuze's sense: not "of lesser quality," but marginalized, disavowed by the hegemonic ideology, or dealing with a "lower," less dignified topic)? If the minor reference is well chosen, such a procedure can lead to insights which completely shatter and undermine our common perceptions. This is what Marx, among others, did with philosophy and religion (short-circuiting philosophical speculation through the lens of political economy, that is to say, economic speculation); this is what Freud and Nietzsche did with morality (short-circuiting the highest ethical notions through the lens of the unconscious libidinal economy). What such a reading achieves is not a simple "desublimation," a reduction of the higher intellectual content to its lower economic or libidinal cause; the aim of such an approach is, rather, the inherent decentering of the interpreted text, which brings to light its "unthought," its disavowed presuppositions and consequences.

And this is what "Short Circuits" wants to do, again and again. The underlying premise of the series is that Lacanian psychoanalysis is a privileged instrument of such an approach, whose purpose is to illuminate a standard text or ideological formation, making it readable in a totally new way—the long history of Lacanian interventions in philosophy, religion, the arts (from the visual arts to the cinema, music, and literature), ideology, and politics justifies this premise. This, then, is not a new series of books on psychoanalysis, but a series of "connections in the Freudian field"—of short Lacanian interventions in art, philosophy, theology, and ideology.

"Short Circuits" intends to revive a practice of reading which confronts a classic text, author, or notion with its own hidden presuppositions, and thus reveals its disavowed truth. The basic criterion for the texts that will be published is that they effectuate such a theoretical short circuit. After reading a book in this series, the reader should not simply have learned something new: the point is, rather, to make him or her aware of another—disturbing—side of something he or she knew all the time.

Slavoj Žižek

THE ODD ONE IN

INTRODUCTION

It may come as little surprise to say that comedy is an extremely difficult subject of investigation—not only because of the multiplicity of various techniques and procedures involved in its process, but also because this process is in constant motion. Indeed, this irresistible motion is one of the key features of comedy, which is why it seems so difficult to pin it down with concepts and definitions. Moreover, comedy lives in the same world as its definitions (in a much more emphatic sense than this could be said for other genres), and is quite capable of its own definitions as material to be submitted to further comic treatment, turned upside down, or inside out. . . .

In this respect—and following Hegel on this point—the argument of this book is that comic subjectivity proper does not reside in the subject making the comedy, nor in the subjects or egos that appear in it, but in this very incessant and irresistible, all-consuming movement. Comic subjectivity is the very movement of comedy. However, movement is not the whole story of comedy. Stumbling, interruptions, punctuations, discontinuities, all kinds of fixations and passionate attachments are the other side of this same movement, and constitute a—not exactly objective but, rather, object-related—facet of comedy. It is with the scissors of this double perspective that this essay ventures to conceptualize the phenomenon of comedy and of the comical.

Philosophy's relationship to comedy is not exactly a simple story, although it contains itself some elements of comedy, starting with the disappearance of the book that might have inaugurated philosophy's more canonical interest in comedy. Thanks to Umberto Eco's best-selling novel *The Name of the Rose* (and the movie based on it), everybody knows about the second book of Aristotle's *Poetics*, in which the philosopher discussed comedy and laughter, and which is unfortunately lost. Would philosophy's often contemptuous attitude towards comedy be any different if it were not lost? Be this as it may, the plot of Eco's story revolves around the "fact" that one copy of the book did survive in a medieval monastic library, where a fanatical monk, Jorge, has made it his mission to prevent the rest of the world from learning about it and reading it. When he can no longer ensure this, he burns down the library and the book with it. Jorge is convinced that laughter is Satan's invention, undermining all firm religious beliefs. If the contents of Aristotle's book on comedy were to become generally known, this would destroy the very foundations of the Christian order. Jorge's adversary and the hero of the story, the enlightened monk William of Baskerville, defends laughter as an essential feature of humankind, seeing Christianity, as a cultural-intellectual enterprise, threatened precisely by fanaticism such as Jorge's.

Let me say immediately that this book does not share the ideological coordinates of this division, which is much too simplistic in its opposition between the rigid fanaticism of ideology and a playfully ironic ease as its worst enemy. Indeed, one can easily show that ironic distance and laughter often function as an internal condition of all true ideology, which is characterized by the fact that it tends to avoid direct "dogmatic" repression, and has a firm hold on us precisely where we feel most free and autonomous in our actions. This point has already been made apropos of Eco's novel:

> Laughter is a condition of ideology. It provides us with the distance, the very space in which ideology can take its full swing. It is only with laughter that we become ideological subjects, withdrawn from the immediate pressure of ideological claims to a free enclave. It is only when we laugh and breathe freely that ideology truly has a hold on us—it is only here that it starts functioning fully as ideology, with the specifically ideological means, which are supposed to assure our free consent and the appearance of spontaneity, eliminating the need for the non-ideological means of outside constraint. (Dolar 1986, p. 307)

It is very important to keep this point in mind, especially in times when freedom and free will, humor, a "positive attitude," and a distance towards all ideologies have become the principal mode of the dominant ideology. The humanist-romantic presentation of comedy as intellectual resistance in the form of keeping a distance to all that is going on around us is not at all what will interest us in comedy. If a truly subversive edge of comedy exists—as I believe it does—it is to be sought elsewhere.

In the contemporary ideological climate it has become imperative that we perceive all the terrible things that happen to us as ultimately something positive—say as a precious experience that will bear fruit in our future life. Negativity, lack, dissatisfaction, unhappiness, are perceived more and more as moral faults—worse, as a corruption at the level of our very being or bare life. There is a spectacular rise of what we might call a bio-morality (as well as morality of feelings and emotions), which promotes the following fundamental axiom: a person who feels good (and is happy) is a good person; a person who feels bad is a bad person. It is this short circuit between the immediate feelings/sensations and the moral value that gives its specific color to the contemporary ideological rhetoric of happiness. This is very efficient, for who dares to raise her voice and say that as a matter of fact, she is not happy, and that she can't manage to—or, worse, doesn't even care to—transform all the disappointments of her life into a positive experience to be invested in the future?

There is an important difference between this and the classical entrepreneur formula according to which we are always broadly responsible for our failures and misfortunes. This classical formula still implies a certain interval between what we are and the symbolic value of our success. It implies that, at least in principle, we could have acted otherwise, but didn't (and are hence responsible for our failures or lack of happiness). The bio-morality mentioned above is replacing the classical notion of responsibility with the notion of a damaged, corrupt being: the unhappy and the unsuccessful are somehow corrupt already on the level of their bare life, and all their erroneous actions or nonactions follow from there with an inexorable necessity. In other words, the problem is not simply that success and efficiency have become the supreme values of our late capitalist society (as we often hear from critics of this society)—there is nothing particularly new in this; social promotion of success (defined in different ways) has existed since time immemorial. The problem is, rather, that success is becoming almost a biological notion, and thus the foundation of a genuine racism of successfulness. The poorest and the most miserable are no longer perceived as a socioeconomic class, but almost as a *race* of their own, as a special form of life. We are indeed witnessing a spectacular rise of racism or, more precisely, of "racization." This is to say that we are no longer simply dealing with racism in its traditional sense of hatred towards other races, but also and above all with a production of (new) races based on economic, political, and class differences and factors, as well as with the segregation based on these differences. If traditional racism tended to socialize biological features—that is, directly translate them into cultural and symbolic points of a given social order—contemporary racism works in the opposite direction. It tends to "naturalize" the differences and features produced by the sociosymbolic order. This is also what can help us to understand the ideological rise of the theme of private life, as well as of lifestyles and habits.

To take a simple example: if a "successful artist" is invited as a guest on a TV show, the focus is practically never on her work, but instead on the way she lives, on her everyday habits, on what she enjoys, and so on. This is not simply a voyeuristic curiosity; it is a procedure that systematically presents us with two elements: "success" on the one side, and the life that corresponds to this success on the other—implying, of course, a strong and immediate equivalence between the two. The objective surplus, the materialized work itself, is eliminated at the very outset. In other words, our ways of life, our habits, our feelings, our more or less idiosyncratic enjoyments—all these are no longer simply "private matters" exposed to scrutiny to satisfy our curiosity. They are one of the crucial cultural catalysts through which all kinds of socioeconomic and ideological differences are being gradually transformed into "human differences," differences at the very core of our being, which makes it possible for them to become the ground of a new racism. This is the process that aims at establishing an immediate connection between being ("bare life") and a socioeconomic value.

We are thus witnessing a massive and forceful naturalization of economic, political, and other social differences, and this naturalization is itself a politico-ideological process *par excellence*. As I said above, "naturalization" involves above all the promotion of a belief in an immediate character of these differences—that is to say, in their being organically related to life as such, or to existing reality in general. I could also put this in the following way: the contemporary discourse which likes to promote and glorify the gesture of distancing oneself from all Ideologies and Projects (as the Ideologies of others, and because they are necessarily totalitarian or utopian) strives to promote its own reality as completely nonideological. Our present socioeconomic reality is increasingly being presented as an immediate *natural* fact, or fact of nature, and thus a fact to which we can only try to adapt as successfully as possible.

If the imperative of happiness, positive thinking, and cheerfulness is one of the key means of expanding and solidifying this ideological hegemony, one cannot avoid the question of whether promoting comedy is not part of the same process. Is comedy not all about cheerfulness, satisfaction, and "positive feelings"? And is this not why Hollywood is producing huge amounts of "comedy," neatly packaged to suit different audiences: romantic comedies, black comedies, teen comedies, family comedies, blue-collar comedies, white-collar comedies . . . ?

Well, this compulsive entertainment has in fact very little to do with comedy, just as comedy has very little to do with nature (or naturalization), immediacy, and feelings. True, comedy does not view men as an exception to nature, as the point that breaks the very laws of nature—this is more the perspective of tragedy. Yet comedy's frequent reduction of man to (his) nature makes a further comic point about nature itself: nature is far from being as "natural" as we might think, but is itself driven by countless contradictions and discrepancies. As for the question of immediacy:

comedy thrives on all kinds of short circuits that establish an immediate connection between heterogeneous orders. Yet again, the immediacy that comedy thus puts forward is not that of a smooth, imperceptible passing of one into another, but that of a material cut between them. If we think of the simplest examples of this procedure (like the one frequent in the Marx Brothers' comedies when, say, A says "Give me a break!" and B pulls a brake out of his pocket), is it not that its fundamental lesson is always this: the only genuine immediate link between these two things is the very cut between them? And as for the question of comedy's nonaffinity with our subjective feelings and emotions—this point has been systematically made in literature on comedy, and is splendidly epitomized by Horace Walpole's remark: "This world is a comedy to those that think, a tragedy to those that feel." Yet this divorce of comedy and feelings is not simply comedy's way of keeping a distance from feelings, but above all its way of introducing a distance (or nonimmediacy) into the feelings themselves. This is especially interesting in the case of happiness: comedies have very ingenious ways of showing us that happiness can indeed be largely independent of how we feel. . . . In other words: there has been some philosophical discussion lately about the difference between what people think they feel and what they really feel. One of the fundamental axioms of what is now officially called "happiness studies" is that there is no difference between the two. In this respect, comedy definitely aligns itself with the opposite camp, which insists that it often happens that we don't know how we really feel, and that emotions (far from constituting a direct insight into the Real of the subject) can lie and be as deceptive as anything else.[1]

A good comedy is—and has always been—a fairly rare thing. And perhaps there is nothing more foreign and hostile to the comic spirit than precisely a climate that praises so highly all sorts of entertainment, promotes happiness as its Master-Signifier, and relies on the immediacy of our feelings as the ground for an ideological immediacy/naturalization of different sociosymbolic relationships. It is as if the imperative of entertainment, "positive thinking," and immediacy were blocking the very heart of comedy, its sparkle, and had blunted the edge on which both comedy and our sensibility to it live and thrive. It is the (im)modest ambition of this book to conceptually revive this edge. Thus the reader should not expect a study of comedy along the lines of a history and theory of literature, or an attempt at a systematic representation of its different modes and authors. Instead, this work is an attempt to bring forward some strong conceptual points made by the practice of comedy, which I believe to be of crucial importance not only for our "understanding" of comedy, but for philosophy and (critical) thinking in general.

The following terminological clarification is perhaps called for. The word "comedy" is frequently used as a general name for (almost) everything that is funny, as a label that covers several different, more specific modes of comedy, such as jokes, irony, humor, and so on. Although I also use the word comedy to designate the comic genre in general (which can include all these modes as well as some others), there is also a much more specific way in which the terms "comedy" and "comical" are used in this book. Its presupposition is a profound conceptual conviction that the "comical" is itself a specific mode of "comedy" (in the broad sense), different from the procedures of jokes, irony, and humor taken in their specificity. In other words, the accent is above all on the specificity of the comical as a singular form of "funniness" at work in comedies that can be distinguished from some other forms. The difference between comedy and jokes is discussed directly and at considerable length, which is not so much the case with other neighboring concepts. This is mostly due to the fact that my aim was to bring out the specificity of the comical, so to speak, from itself, and not so much by the procedure of systematically distinguishing it from its neighboring phenomena. Another reason is that, despite their specificity, the boundaries of these phenomena are in fact often blurred or, perhaps more precisely, these different phenomena of funniness have a funny way of appearing, in their very singularity, within the field of each other. This is why it can make sense to speak, say, of "comic irony," which is not different only from "tragic irony," but also from "ironic irony."

Philosophy and comedy—what good might come from this encounter? What is the use of "philosophizing comedy"? Indeed, there is probably not much use in it, but this is precisely where comedy might come to philosophy's rescue. "Philosophizing" is often viewed as a fairly useless enterprise: "Stop philosophizing and get back to serious work!" or, as the latest version of this imperative goes, "Stop philosophizing and start enjoying yourself!" are just two expressions that remind us of that. Yet it is precisely this refusal to stop when things no longer serve any immediate purpose, and seem to run way off their mark (to—we may hope—hit it in another, unexpected place), that philosophy shares with comedy; this is why "Stop that comedy!" is another expression of the kind mentioned above. To the question: "Why try to conceptualize comedy if it is notoriously recalcitrant to conceptualization?" one should thus reply with another question: Why stop philosophy's most precious intrinsic comedy when it comes to comedy?

PART I

THE CONCRETE UNIVERSAL

THE ABSOLUTE ON THE COUCH

There is little doubt that among classical philosophers, Hegel was the one who valued comedy and the comic spirit most highly. In the *Phenomenology of Spirit* he considers comedy to be the most accomplished spiritual work of art, elaborating on it—briefly, but concisely—within the triad epos–tragedy–comedy that concludes the section on "Religion in the Form of Art." The fact that Hegel discusses art within the section on religion demands some preliminary remarks concerning the structure of the *Phenomenology* and the status of the discussion of art in it. Without entering into a detailed account of the construction of this unique philosophical work (which is still subject to considerable debate, partly because Hegel changed his original plans as he went along), let me just point out some general outlines. The *Phenomenology* falls into two big triads. The first is formed by sections on Consciousness, Self-Consciousness, and Reason; the second by sections on Spirit, Religion, and Absolute Knowledge. I will leave the first triad aside. We thus have Spirit, Religion, and Absolute Knowledge in a triad that seems to represent an almost caricature peak of idealism, and to embody everything that a major part of contemporary philosophy has been—and still is—fighting against. Yet in this theater of the Spirit, Hegel gives us more than one comic surprise, bearing witness to the fact that, all in all, Spirit is very much a matter of comedy.

For Hegel, Spirit is nothing other than the world; as such, it is most material—it is, so to speak, a materialist reversal of the movement Consciousness–Self-Consciousness–Reason, where all shapes of consciousness are still only "abstract forms of it" (Hegel 1977, p. 264). Reason becomes Spirit when it is conscious of itself as its own world, and of the world as itself. The shapes or figures (*Gestalten*) of the Spirit are now "real Spirits, actualities in the strict meaning of the word, and instead of being shapes merely of consciousness, are shapes of the world" (ibid., p. 265). In a word, Spirit is reason as materially existing, above all in the ethical life and practices of a community. The section on Spirit thus covers (from this new standpoint, which is the standpoint

Institutions

13

of community) history, starting from Greek Antiquity (the immediacy of Spirit—the ethical order); it continues with the process of Bildung, Culture, where the world of the Spirit breaks in two and is alienated from itself (this is where the history of Christianity comes in), up to the point where (after the Enlightenment and the French Revolution) Spirit appears in the shape of "Morality" as "Spirit that is certain of itself," Spirit that has done away with the Other world. This concludes the section on Spirit. Here, on the threshold of the section on Religion, there is a very significant shift of perspective. If, in the section on Spirit, the emphasis is on how Spirit (as world) appears to consciousness, and how the latter conceives it, in the section on Religion the emphasis is on the question of how Spirit (or the Absolute) conceives itself. We are dealing with two different emphases: the duality or tension between "in itself" and "for consciousness," of course, remains, and the way consciousness perceives or grasps the Absolute remains, also in the section on Religion, an important driving force of the dialectical movement. For the sake of better conceptual clarity, however, we can sharpen things a little and say: consciousness and the Absolute, which are indispensable agents in both sections, exchange roles. If, prior to this section, the principal role belonged to consciousness which, in the spirit of the world, had to come to its own Absolute, the main role now goes to the Absolute, which has to achieve its self-consciousness. The section on Religion is thus a peculiar Divine Comedy, in which what is at stake is, so to speak, a "consciousness-raising" of the Absolute itself (that is to say, of the Absolute as materially existing in different forms of religion and art). The question is no longer simply that of how consciousness conceives of or sees the Absolute, but also of how the Absolute sees itself. It is this second, rather unique perspective that prompted one of the great interpreters of Hegel, Jean Hyppolite, to suggest that in the section on Religion we are no longer dealing just with "phenomenology of spirit" but also, and above all, with its "noumenology" (Hyppolite 1978, pp. 522–523).

As for the status of the section on Religion (in which the discussion of comedy also appears), we could say that Hegel's paradoxical—and ultimately atheist—wager lies in the following: it is not enough that consciousness comes to know that it is itself the source and the drive of that Absolute Spirit which, from a certain point on, appears to it as its unattainable Beyond, its Other (and that it reappropriates it or declares its illusory character, the fact that it is but a product of consciousness itself). Hegel's point is that Absolute Spirit as the product of consciousness is, precisely as this product, something real, something that has material and historical existence. (One could say that, in this respect, Hegel anticipates the Althusserian thesis about the materiality of ideology—are not what Althusser calls "Ideological State Apparatuses" precisely one of the forms in which spirit exists as the world?)

And this is the cause of the ultimate impotence of the reason of Enlightenment, the reason which knows that the Other (world) does not exist, yet remains powerless in the face of all the practices (including its own) which, in spite of that knowledge, still keep manifesting some form of religious belief. "*Je sais bien, mais quand même . . .* (I know very well, but nevertheless . . .)" is a quasi-universal paradigm of the post-Enlightenment belief which, to a large extent, we still share today. At stake here is precisely the paradigm of the following, most insightful joke: a man believes that he is a grain of seed. He is taken to a mental institution, where the doctors do their best finally to convince him that he is not a grain, but a man. No sooner has he left the hospital than he comes back, very scared, claiming that there is a chicken outside the door, and he is afraid that it will eat him. "Dear fellow," says his doctor, "you know very well that you are not a grain of seed, but a man." "Of course I know that," replies the patient, "but does the chicken?" In a word: it is not enough that we know how things really stand; in a certain sense, things themselves have to realize how they stand. In the context of the confrontation between Enlightenment and religion, this joke could perhaps be reformulated as follows. In the enlightened society of, say, revolutionary terror, a man is put in prison because he believes in God. By various means, but above all by means of an enlightened explanation, he is brought to the knowledge that God does not exist. When he is freed, the man comes running back and explains how scared he is of being punished by God. Of course he knows God does not exist, but does God know it, too?

In a certain sense, the whole section on Religion in the *Phenomenology of Spirit* represents Hegel's most extraordinary attempt at staging this other movement in which Absolute Spirit itself has to reach the conclusion that it does not exist (outside the concrete consciousness of people and of the world). This section is thus the other (or the obverse) side of the phenomenology of spirit; it is a paradoxical, almost postmodern story about how the narrative of the experience of consciousness is seen and read by what this same experience of consciousness produces in its historic movement. And—if we refer again to the joke above—in this perspective, the "Absolute Knowledge" that follows the chapter on religion and concludes the *Phenomenology* is nothing but a paradoxical coincidence of the knowledge of the patient with the knowledge of the chicken.

Here we can, of course, note a crucial affinity between this double movement and what is at stake in psychoanalysis. In psychoanalysis (if it is worthy of its name) the main problem also does not lie simply in the subject becoming conscious of her unconscious, of all that (often painfully) determines her actions and experiences. This is insufficient: the main problem is precisely how to shift and change the very symbolic and imaginary structures in which this unconscious is embodied outside herself, in the manner and rituals of her conduct, speech, relations to others—in certain situations that keep "happening" to her. In short, it is not simply that in analysis the subject has to shift her position (or even adapt herself); the major part of the analytic work consists precisely in shifting the external practices, in moving all those "chickens" in which the subject's unconscious (and her relation to herself) are externalized. And one of the major obstacles that can occur in analysis is precisely that the subject can become all too eager to change herself and her perception of the world, convinced that in analysis she will experience a kind of intimate revelation as a result of which everything will be different and easier when she reenters the world. In other words, the subject is ready to do quite a lot, change radically, if only she can remain unchanged in the Other (in the Symbolic as the external world in which, to put it in Hegel's terms, the subject's consciousness of herself is embodied, materialized as something that still does not know itself as consciousness). In this case, belief in the Other (in the modern form of believing that the Other does not know) is precisely what helps to maintain the same state of things, regardless of all subjective mutations and permutations. The subject's universe will really change only at the moment when she attains the knowledge that the Other knows (that it does not exist).

What Lacan and Hegel share in this respect is that they both take this dimension of the Other extremely seriously—not as a subjective illusion or spell that could be broken simply by saying out loud that "the Other doesn't exist" (just consider how this common theoretical mantra coexists perfectly well with all sorts of secret or not-so-secret beliefs), but as something which, despite its nonexistence, has considerable material effects in which it does exist.

This is why, for both Hegel and Lacan, the real point at which something in this relationship can be effectively shifted is not the abolition of Otherness, or its absorption into the subject, but the coincidence of the lack in the subject with the lack in the Other. In other words, what is needed is the encounter of the two entities at a very precise (or precisely right) point of their topology. This is a short circuit of internal and external, not an elimination of the one or the other. For this short circuit or local overlapping of the two to occur, work on the subject, as an internal work on consciousness, is not enough; work on the Other is also needed. In psychoanalysis, the condition of this work on the Other is transference. And transference is ultimately nothing but the subject's trust in her own sameness or identity, functioning outside her, in the Other. This trust or "credit" is needed, because the subject has no immediate control over what her sameness does, and how it speaks in this exteriority.

In this feature we could recognize a properly comic dimension of analytic experience. I am referring to the autonomy of the (subject's) sameness that is operating "out there," doing all kinds of things, involving the subject in various possible and impossible situations, sometimes very awkward ones. At the moment of entry into analysis the subject is usually experiencing this as a tragic, painful split between the way she perceives herself, her desires, and so on, and the unpleasant things that keep "happening" to her, and constitute the way things are "in reality." And the analyst is not—as is sometimes thought—the authority that simply refers the subject back to herself, pointing out how she is in fact responsible for what is so systematically "happening" to her; the analyst is, rather and above all, the authority that has to give all this "happening" the time (and the space) to come to the subject. This could be one of the main reasons for the long duration of analysis, for the precipitation of knowledge does not really solve anything: we can come to know what there is to know quite soon in this process, yet this insight of knowledge is not enough; the work of analysis is also needed, the work that is not simply the work of analyzing (things), but much more the work of repetition, work as "entropy." In analysis, the subject very often rushes in different directions, each time expecting to find some salutary knowledge, some secret formula that will deliver her from her pain. And as a rule, she comes again and again, through all these different paths, to the same things, and knowledge that keeps repeating itself. The subject thus often goes along the same paths again and again. Yet this work, in all its entropy, is precisely not empty, it is not wasted time, it is what is needed for knowledge (that can be present from a very early stage) to come to the place of truth.

But let us return to Hegel and the section on Religion, where what comes to the foreground is this other, obverse movement, which can be quite scandalous precisely from the viewpoint of what is usually called religion. Could one not say that an irreducible germ of comedy is involved already in this perspective, where we are dealing not so much with the question of how consciousness perceives the Absolute but, rather, with the question of how the Absolute perceives itself?

A great example of this kind of movement can be found in Chaplin's *The Gold Rush*, in the segment where it is hunger that gets subjected to comical treatment, and where the central role again belongs—to a chicken! Although this time the situation is reversed, and it is the chicken that is scared of being eaten by a madman. Charlie and Big Jim are snowbound and starving in their small hut. Suddenly Big Jim, suffering hallucinations from hunger, imagines that Charlie is a plump chicken and wants to eat him. It is very instructive to learn how this scene of Charlie's metamorphosis, under Big Jim's crazed eyes, into a chicken, evolved during the shooting. For several days the unit shot a version of the scene in which Big Jim simply sees the vision of a fine fat chicken sitting on the table. When he grabs for it, it disappears only to reappear in Charlie's person, whereupon Big Jim chases him around the hut with a knife. And then Charlie came up with a better idea: he ordered a man-size chicken costume, and decided that he would play Big Jim's *fata Morgana* himself. It was with this that the whole comic potential of the scene came to life. Why? Because the scene is no longer constructed simply upon the discrepancy between what Charlie really is and how the other sees him (as a chicken), but adds something else: it brings to light the chickenish properties of the man-Charlie himself. All of a sudden we come to see how Charlie himself, in his habitual Chaplinesque gestures (in the way he flaps his arms, and in his toes-out waddle), displays the "characteristics which exactly coincide with the movements of the chicken" (Robinson 1989, p. 340). It is this short circuit that constitutes the peak of comedy: not simply the fact that Big Jim erroneously sees a chicken when he looks at Charlie, but also the fact that, for all his error, he is somehow right— Charlie does look like a chicken. We could also say: for the solution of this crisis, it is not enough for Big Jim to realize that the chicken he sees in front of him is really his friend—the chicken itself must realize that it is really Charlie Chaplin. A further detail from the shooting that supports this reading is that at some point another actor was substituted in the chicken costume; this didn't work at all, and Chaplin had to take over. As Robinson pointedly remarks: "That actor was only able to be a man in a chicken costume. Chaplin, at will, could be a chicken" (ibid., p. 341).

Before we move on to what Hegel has to say on the subject of comedy, just a few final remarks and orientation points. "Religion in the Form of Art" appears between "Natural Religion," with which the section starts, and "The Revealed Religion," with which it concludes. Given how Hegel situates it within the historical side of the *Phenomenology*, Religion in the form of art covers exclusively the period of Ancient Greece: sculpture, hymn-lyric, and the movement of Cult ("the abstract work of art"), Dionysian celebrations ("the living work of art"), and the Greek epics, tragedy and comedy ("the spiritual work of art"). In this last complex, which interests us, we are thus actually dealing with a very narrow and precise segment of art, represented by the names of Homer (the epics), Aeschylus and Sophocles (tragedy), and Aristophanes (comedy). So, not only does Hegel discuss art in the section on Religion, he is also discussing a very specific moment of art. And we might well ask what we should expect from this kind of overdetermined (by the question of religion) and at the same time extremely limited (in its references) discussion of art. Is it not all too obvious that Hegel simply and skillfully uses certain forms of art to fill in the speculative framework that he develops and constructs independently of them, the framework of self-representation of Absolute Spirit? To a certain extent, this is entirely true. Art is not an immediate subject of discussion, but appears and comes to life in the process of discussing something else. This is not exactly what we might call today an immanent approach to art (although one is often led to wonder what this immanent approach is actually supposed to mean); yet it is not a simple gesture of application either. Hegel does not apply his con-

cepts to different forms of art, but introduces the latter as cases of
concretely existing moments of the concept, and this indirect approach allows him to propose several very precious insights. This
is especially true of his comments on comedy. Thus, in the few
pages dedicated to comedy in the *Phenomenology of Spirit*, we must not
look for some all-encompassing theory of comedy that would allow us, among other things, to distinguish conceptually between
different periods and authors of comedy, as well as different comical procedures that they create and use in their work. What we
will be looking for is something else, something that could be a
very productive starting point for a philosophical discussion of
comedy: what is the singular moment of the Spirit that is at work
in comedy? Instead of trying to deduce a common essence from
the multiplicity of different comedies, we will rather embark,
with Hegel, on a journey of philosophical construction of the
"comic perspective," which, as I hope to show, not only signifi-
cantly challenges and undermines many of the received ideas on
what comedy is and how it works, but also invites a broader discussion of several central points of religion, philosophy, and psychoanalysis, especially those related to claims about human
finitude, which will be addressed (and also questioned) in the last
chapter of this Part.

THE UNIVERSAL-AT-WORK

If we are properly to appreciate Hegel's comments on comedy, it is now necessary briefly to sketch out his remarks on the epic and on tragedy, which immediately precede and lead to the discussion of comedy.

The key issue of the entire section on the spiritual work of art is representation. It is precisely the (gradual) abolition of representation that puts the three genres of epic, tragedy, and comedy in a succession that is not simply historical, but also dialectical. The starting point of the "spiritual work of art" is a split or duality that has several names: human/divine, subject (self)/substance, contingency/necessity, individual/universal, self-consciousness/external existence, essential world/world of action. We are thus dealing with a rather brutal duality of the world where notions such as essence, substance, necessity, universality (and the corresponding entities—gods) stand opposed to those of appearance, subjectivity, contingency, individuality (and, of course, the entities that correspond to these notions—human beings). The key question concerns the relationship between these couples, and it is precisely with this question that the destiny of representation will be played out. All three forms of spiritual art mediate—each in its own way—the terms of this duality.

In the universe of the epic we thus have, on the one hand, ordinary people and, on the other, the gods, the epic being precisely a "synthetic linking together" of the two terms, their "mixture" (*Vermischung*). What characterizes the formal structure of the epic is, first, that the content (the relationship between the human and the divine) is, for the first time, *presented* to consciousness (that is, represented). The mode of the epic is thus the mode of narrative as representation, and the process of mixture appears at that level. How? As the mixture of the universal and the individual: the medium of the epic is language, which belongs to the universal, yet—and at the same time—the Minstrel is an individual who, as a subject of this world, produces and bears this language. The extreme of universality, the world of gods, is linked with individuality, with the Minstrel. They are linked through the middle term of particularity, which is simply the nation embodied in its heroes, who are individual men like the Minstrel, yet present and thereby at the same time universal. This is basically the form of syllogism that Hegel recognizes in the epic. At its core, representation is thus nothing but "a synthetic combination of the universal and the individual" (Hegel 1977, p. 441). Yet this combination or linking remains external: the principle of action, which belongs to the subject or the self, is, so to speak, projected onto universal powers (gods) from the outside (that is, from the other side); it is applied to them. The universal powers have the form of individuality and the principle of action: their actions are identical to those of men; universal powers act like humans. But, at the same time, these universal powers remain the universal that withdraws from the connection with the concrete: they are the universal that remains unrestricted in its own specific character (gods are individual gods, set up one against the other, yet their divine existence is independent of individuality). To put it simply: the limitation of this kind of universal is precisely that it is *not really limited* by its own concrete individuality, but remains above it. This, for Hegel, is the weakness (and not, perhaps, the strength) of this universal. It is the kind of universal that "through the invincible elasticity of its unity effaces the atomistic singleness of the doer and his constructions, preserves itself in its purity and dissolves everything individual in its fluid nature" (ibid., p. 442). Concrete subjects, with their determinate nature, cannot find themselves in this purity. As such, this universal and its powers remain a "void of necessity" that floats *above* the heroes and everything else.

We now come to the next form of spiritual work of art, tragedy, which—far from being an antithesis of the epic, as one sometimes too automatically expects from Hegel—assembles more closely together the dispersed moments of the inner essential world and the world of action. In Greek tragedy, the language is no longer simply a universal medium of representation; it ceases to be narrative and enters into the content: instead of being spoken about, the heroes now speak for themselves, they are the speakers.

So the content ceases to be representative, although, as we shall see, the moment of representation remains present in tragedy on another level. The performance displays to the audience—who are also spectators—"self-conscious human beings who know their rights and purposes, the power and the will of their specific nature and now how to assert them" (Hegel 1977, p. 444). These are now characters that exist as actual human beings who impersonate the heroes and portray them not in the form of narrative, but in the actual speech and action of the actors themselves. In other words, via the actors, the universal itself starts to speak. We could say that if the epic introduces and practices the form of narrating the Essence, tragedy introduces and practices the form of (en)acting or staging it.

If we link the historical and the structural perspectives, the "birth of tragedy" presents us with real human beings, the actors, who put on their masks and represent the essence with the help of the mask. The self of an individual (the actor) puts on a mask and, with it, puts on the character he is playing. In this way we come to a new mode of representation, which is not narrative (and in this sense figurative, imaginary), but is linked to the Real of the mask itself as the gap or interval between the actor and the character. The mask as such has no content, it is more like the pure surface— or, most literally, it is the interface—that separates the self of the actor from his stage character as (represented) essence. When the actor puts on the mask, he is no longer himself; in the mask, he brings to life the (universal) essence he represents. This means, however, that here also the essence ultimately exists only as the universal moment, separated by the mask from the concrete and actual self, and that as such this essence is still not actual. The self appears merely as assigned to the characters.

The union between self-consciousness and substance or faith thus remains external; it is "a hypocrisy, . . . the hero who appears before the onlookers splits up into his mask and the actor, into the person in the play and the actual self" (Hegel 1977, p. 450). We could also say that the actor, who is there to represent the essence, has to make us forget his actual self, and see only the sublime character as essence. All that can remind us of the actual existence of the actor behind the mask (for instance, his bodily functions, slips, and so on) is disturbing to the effect of representation; it is bad representation, bad performance.

Now, how do things stand with comedy? There are many authors who see in comedy precisely the emphasis on this other, human side of representation which is a reminder of the physical residue that the mask can never completely sublimate or absorb, a reminder of an irreducible (real) refusal of the symbolic gesture of representation, a kind of "objection of conscience" that finds its voice in comedy. Unlike those authors who see comedy as representing or giving voice to the other side of representation, to its failure, Hegel goes considerably further and introduces a rather spectacular shift of perspective that one could formulate as follows: the comic character is not the physical remainder of the symbolic representation of essence; it is *this very essence as physical*. And this is precisely why, according to Hegel, the comic work of art does away with representation. How, and what does this mean?

With (Greek) tragedy and its mode of representation, we had, on the one side, abstract universality and Fate, and on the other, self-consciousness, the individual self that represented this fate as a stage character. With (Greek) comedy, says Hegel, "the actual self of the actor coincides with what he impersonates (with his stage character), just as the spectator is completely at home in the drama performed before him and sees himself playing in it" (Hegel 1977, p. 452). This passage is crucial, and requires commentary. We should not understand Hegel to be claiming that, in comedy, actors no longer act, but simply appear as themselves. A performance is still a performance, as Hegel himself is careful to point out. What loses the form of representation (that is, the form of being separated from the actual self) are universal powers, gods, Fate, essence. In comedy, "the *individual self* is the negative power through which and in which the gods, as also their moment, . . . vanish" (ibid., p. 452). However, continues Hegel, the individual self is not the emptiness of this disappearance but, on the contrary, preserves itself in this very nothingness, abides with itself and is the sole actuality. Through the fact that it is individual consciousness in the certainty of itself that exhibits itself as this absolute power, it has lost the form of something (re)*presented to consciousness*, something altogether *separate* from consciousness and alien to it (like the content of the epic or the essential characters in tragedy). This emphasis is absolutely essential. Absolute powers lose the form of things represented by appearing themselves as subjects or as concrete beings.

In order to unravel this highly condensed speculative argument, I propose the following reading. When comedy exposes to laughter, one after another, all the figures of the universal essence and its powers (gods, morals, state institutions, universal ideas, and so on) it does so, of course, from the standpoint of the concrete and the subjective; and, on the face of it, we can indeed get the impression that in comedy, the individual, the concrete, the contingent, and the subjective are opposing and undermining the universal, the necessary, the substantial (as their other). And this is, to be sure, the view that a great many authors propose as the paradigm of comedy. Hegel's point, however, is that in this very "work of the negative" (through which comic subjectivity appears) comedy produces its own necessity, universality, and substantiality (it is itself the only "absolute power"), and it does so by revealing the figures of the "universal in itself" as something that is, in the end, utterly empty and contingent.[1]

Comedy is not the undermining of the universal, but its (own) reversal into the concrete; it is not an objection to the universal, but the concrete labor or work of the universal itself. Or, to put it in a single slogan: *comedy is the universal at work*. This is a universal which is no longer (re)presented as being in action, but *is* in action. In other words, "the negative power through which and in which the gods vanish" is precisely the power which has been previously (in the mode of representation) attributed to gods, and has now become the acting subject. To recapitulate: in the epic, the

subject narrates the universal, the essential, the absolute; in tragedy, the subject enacts or stages the universal, the essential, the absolute; in comedy, the subject is (or becomes) the universal, the
essential, the absolute. Which is also to say that the universal, the
essential, the absolute become the subject.

In comedy, says Hegel, the *Self is the absolute Being*. In comic consciousness, "all divine being returns, or it is the complete alienation of substance" (Hegel 1977, p. 455). That is to say: in comic
consciousness, the substance is not alienated from the self or the
subject (as it is in the "unhappy consciousness"), it is alienated
from itself, and this is the only way it comes to self-consciousness
and to life in the strict meaning of the word. Comedy is not the
story of the alienation of the subject, it is the story of the alienation of the substance, which has become the subject.

It is hardly possible to overemphasize this crucial point. At first
sight, it seems that in comedy all that is concrete, and belongs to
the content, refutes/rebuts the universal-formal. There is no sacred thing or solidity that comedy could not rock to its foundations. Just think, for instance, of Monty Python's *The Meaning of Life*:
a delirious comedy in which we, so to speak, laugh at all human
certainties and universal values, one after another. Yet Hegel's
point is that this movement of revealing the universal as a "play of
the caprice of chance individuality" is possible only through a radical shift in the fundamental structure: in comedy, the universal is
on the side of undermining the "universal"; the comic movement, its "negative power," *is the movement of the universal itself* (and
precisely as *movement*, this universal is also the subject).

This also helps us to explain one rather paradoxical feature of
comedy; "paradoxical," since it appears to be in contradiction
with the generally recognized materialism of comedy, its emphasis on the concrete and on the Real of human limitations and
deficiencies. The comic universe is, as a rule, the universe of the
indestructible (this feature is brought to its climax in cartoons, but
is also present, in a more subtle way, in most comedies). Regardless of all accidents and catastrophes (physical as well as psychic

or emotional) that befall comic characters, they always rise from the chaos perfectly intact, and relentlessly go on pursuing their goals, chasing their dreams, or simply being themselves. It seems that nothing can really get to them, which somehow contradicts the realistic view of the world that comedy is supposed to promote. To take a kind of archetypal example: a toffee-nosed baron slips on a banana peel (thus demonstrating that even he is subject to the laws of gravity), yet the next instant he is up again and walking around arrogantly, no less sure of the highness of His Highness, until the next accident that will again try to "ground" him, and so on and so on. (Take, for example, Sir John Falstaff in Shakespeare's comedy *The Merry Wives of Winsdor*.)

How are we to understand this consistent feature of comedy, the surprising fact that in this genre of the concrete, the concrete does not seem really to get to people? As a matter of fact, the answer is quite simple. The constellation described looks like a paradox as long as we do not notice that in comedy, the abstract and the concrete have switched places at the very outset. What do we mean by this? Let us stay with the archetypal character of a buffoonish baron who implacably believes in his aristocratic superiority, although throughout the comedy he stumbles, so to speak, from one muddy puddle to another. We have only to think about it a little in order to see that what we are dealing with here is in no way an abstract-universal idea (belief in the elevated nature of his own aristocratic personality) undermined, for our amusement, by intrusions of material reality. Or, to put it differently, we are not dealing with an abstract perfection, belied by human weaknesses and limitations to which this VIP is nonetheless subjected. On the contrary, is it not only too obvious that the capital human weakness here—what is most human, concrete, and realistic—is precisely the baron's unshakeable belief in himself and his own importance: that is to say, his presumptuousness? This is the feature that makes him "human," not the fact that he falls into a muddy puddle or slips on a banana peel. Banana peels, muddy puddles, and all the other devices through which reality reminds the comic character of its existence are ultimately much more abstract (and, let us not forget, often much more unrealistic) than the baron's very vivid and palpable belief in his own aristocratic Self. And, of course, we should not overlook the fact that what is really funny and makes us laugh most in our archetypal (imaginary) comedy is not simply that the baron falls into the puddle but, much more, that he *rises* from it and goes about his business as if nothing has happened. The puddle itself is thus not the site of the concrete reality (in which anybody turns out to be only human), but one of the props or devices through which the very concreteness or humanity of the concept itself—in our case, the concept of baronage or aristocracy—is processed, crystallized, and concretized. In other words, what is indestructible in comedies and comic characters is this very movement of concrete universality.

Here we also come to an important distinction between, I would venture to say, true and false comedies (a distinction that broadly corresponds to the distinction between subversive and conservative). It is not a question of *what* (which content) is subjected to comical treatment—Mother Teresa, Lenin, machismo, feminism, the institution of the family, or the life of a homosexual couple—it is a question of the mode of the comic processing itself. False, conservative comedies are those where the abstract-universal and the concrete do not change places and do not produce a short circuit between them; instead, the concrete (where "human weaknesses" are situated) remains external to the universal, and at the same time invites us to recognize and accept it as the indispensable companion of the universal, its necessary physical support. The paradigm of these comedies is simply the following: the aristocrat (or king, or judge, or priest, or any other character of symbolic stature) is *also* a man (who snores, farts, slips, and is subject to the same physical laws as other mortals). The emphasis is, of course, precisely on "also": the concrete and the universal coexist, the concrete being the indispensable grounding of the universal. This is the great wisdom of those comedies which actually get stuck halfway down the path to the comical: we have to consider and accept the material, physical, concrete, and human aspect of things, otherwise we will be carried into a dangerous abstract ideality, extremism, if not even fanaticism (for instance, that of forgetting our own limitations and our mortality)—as if this perspective of combining the universal and the concrete, the aristocrat and the man, were not in itself utterly abstract. This mechanism runs out of steam precisely at the point where true comedy begins, and leaves all the universals, the human side of which it tries to expose, fundamentally untouched in their abstract purity, since the dirt is absorbed by the human side, which is then forgiven as belonging to the "necessary evil." (Thus, for example, in this case the comedy of baronage would never be exactly the comedy of baronage as such, but always that of its contingent bearers, particular individuals, who are "only human.") This kind of comedy remains caught in an abstract dualism of the concrete and the universal and, much as it may emphasize the side of the concrete, this concrete remains but one element in the constellation of the universal versus the concrete, which is itself purely abstract. The conservatism of this paradigm springs, of course, from the fact that it offers the audience, via the "human" aspect, an identification with the baron as ego-ideal, which as such remains not only untouched, but even reinforced. We identify with heroes' weaknesses, yet their higher calling (or universal symbolic function) remains all the more the object of respect and fascination (instead of being the object of comic laughter).

So what, in this respect, is a true comedy? Comedy which does not try to seduce us into deceptive familiarity with the fact that His Highness is *also*, at the same time, or "on the other hand," as human as the rest of us? A true comedy about a presumptuous baron has to produce the following formula in all its materiality: an aristocrat who believes that he is really and intrinsically an aristocrat is, *in this very belief*, a common silly human. In other words: a true comedy about aristocracy has to play its cards in such a way that the very universal aspect of this concept produces its own humanity, corporeality, subjectivity. Here, the body is not an indispensable basis of the soul; an inflexible belief in one's own baronage is precisely the point where the soul itself is as *corporeal* as possible. The concrete body of the baron, which repeatedly falls into the puddle of human weaknesses, is not simply the empirical body that lies flat in the mud, but much more the belief in his baronage, his "baronness." This "baronness" is the real comic object, produced by comedy as the quintessence of the universal itself. To put it in psychoanalytic terms: here, the ego-ideal itself turns out to be the partial (comical) object, and ceases to be something with which we identify via the identification with one of the partial features of its reverse side. The ego-ideal directly is a human weakness—which is to say that, in this kind of comedy, the process of identification with the partial feature is, by virtue of its comic character, always also the process of disidentification. The point is not that an aristocrat is also an ordinary man. He is an ordinary man precisely *as an aristocrat,* at the very peak of his aristocracy. Here we should recall Lacan's famous remark that a lunatic is not some poor chap who believes that he is a king; a lunatic is a king who believes that he really is a king. Does this not hold even more for comedy? It is not some poor chap who believes himself to be a king who is comical (this is rather pathetic), but a king who believes that he really is a king.

A very good recent example of this kind of comic procedure of disidentification is *Borat*. The constitutive movement of almost every episode of Borat's apprenticeship in the "US and A" involves a short circuit between some universal (and acceptable) notion or belief and its obscene other side. Yet the latter does not figure as the other side of what is "universally acceptable," but as its most intimate kernel which is made, by Borat, to explode right before our very eyes. Take the example of the brief but extremely effective gun shop episode. The firearms possession issue in America is split between, on the one hand, the universally proclaimed right to defend oneself and, on the other, louder and louder reminders of its catastrophic side-effects, such as fatal accidents, misuses of easily acquirable guns. . . . Now, what happens in the *Borat* episode is that Borat walks into a (real) gun shop, and asks the guy selling the arms a very straightforward question (in his "Kazakhstanian English"): "What is the best gun to defend from a Jew?" Without so much as a blink, the shop assistant replies: "I would recommend either a 9 mm or a 45." This exchange is simultaneously both shocking and comical, because of the smoothness with which the rather spectacular short circuit between the "right to self-defense" (by possession of firearms) and the taste for "shooting Jews" passes unnoticed by the assistant. And, of course, the point is precisely that the two *cannot in fact* be dissociated.

Thus, the difference between subversive and conservative comedies does not lie in their content, in what is subjected to the comical procedure. This also means that we will not find it where some authors, following a sort of ascetic ethics, place it: in other words—and to put it simply—in the question of whether we are making fun of ourselves and our own beliefs, or of others and their beliefs. This distinction is invalid for several reasons, but principally for the following one. The direct parody of oneself and one's beliefs can flourish very well within the conservative paradigm of combining the concrete and the universal. It can successfully promote the very ideology whose human side and weaknesses are being exposed. There are plenty of examples in several veins of Hollywood comedy, in which derision of our own beliefs and of the "American way of life" produces the very distance necessary to sustain these very same beliefs and this very same way of life. Or—an even more obvious example—President Bush and his media strategy of mocking his own presidential self, which of course aims precisely at portraying the inflexible war President as "the guy next door," as a fallible individual who is aware of his faults and imperfections. In this case, the wittiness functions precisely as a way of distancing oneself from one's own concreteness (which, of course, is the very opposite of the primacy of the concrete): one gets evacuated, so to speak, into one's wit or spirit, and the message sent out is that one is something *more* than one's miserable concrete self. The real comedy of George W. Bush can be seen at times when he makes no effort to be funny, but solemnly appears as an American President who believes that he really is an American President. It is at these moments that he comes up with the most comical lines, the collection of which has become an Internet sport. Take a few examples: "You teach a child to read, and he or her will be able to pass a literacy test" (Townsend, Tennessee, February 21, 2001). The following, probably the most famous one, is almost as good as the Freud–Heine "famillionaire" joke: "They misunderestimated me" (Bentonville, Arkansas, November 6, 2000).[2] Or one of the more recent ones: "Our enemies are innovative and resourceful, and so are we. They never stop thinking about new ways to harm our country and our people, and neither do we" (Washington, DC, August 5, 2004). Contrary to this, the other kind of Bush humor, with which he likes to demonstrate his ability to laugh at these miracles of wit that he keeps producing, is already a refashioning of the self-undermining power of "Bushisms" themselves into a conservative way of accepting and tolerating pure stupidity.

Comedy is the moment in which substance, necessity, and essence all lose their immediate—and thus abstract—self-identity or coincidence with themselves. This emphasis is important because it reminds us that the end of the mode of representation does not imply a return to immediacy or to an organic fusion of opposites. The substance becomes subject in the moment when, through a split in itself, it starts relating to itself. In this way we come not so much to the abolition of representation but, rather, to its new notion, which is in fact very close to the Lacanian concept of representation. Could we not say that in comedy, one moment of the substance represents the subject for another moment of the substance? If so, we could perhaps answer an objection that might be raised in relation to the Hegelian distinction between comedy and tragedy, as cited above. We saw that, according to Hegel, the main (formal) problem of tragedy is that it preserves the interval between the subject or the self and the character or stage person that the self is representing. With comedy, this interval is supposed to disappear. We might object to this by pointing out that it is precisely in comedy that we find a whole arsenal of various characters that exist quite independently of the concrete subjects, and they are occasionally assumed by these subjects as masks, for the purposes of comedy ("idiotic master," "cunning servant," "miser," "shrew," "tramp". . .). On the other hand, tragedy seems to be much closer to an organic fusion of the actor and his character.

We will answer this objection by clarifying the misunderstanding that generates it. Tragedy can appear as an organic fusion or synthesis of the actor-subject and the character precisely because the subject represents the character (and the better the representation, the more powerful will be the feeling of a fusion of these two, of the individual and the universal). Hegel would entirely agree with this, and he says as much himself. The problem is that, convincing as this fusion-in-representation might be, it still remains exactly that: a fusion of the two, an individual representation of the universal, without reaching the point where one of the two terms would generate the other from within itself, and become this other. To put it more precisely: we are still dealing with the classical mode of representation, a constellation of two elements in which one represents the other. What happens in comedy is that the subject changes its place. The subject is no longer the one who represents something (as actor, and with the help of his mask) and to whom (as spectator) something is represented. Recall Hegel's thesis that in comedy "the actual self of the actor coincides with what he impersonates (with his stage character), just as the spectator is completely at home in the drama performed before him, and sees himself playing in it." This coincidence of the self (the actor) and his character means that the split between these two now moves to and inhabits that character itself (that is, the essence), and it is precisely this inner split that constitutes the place of the subject in the character. This is why, when speaking of comedy, we cannot say that the subject-actor represents a (comic) character for the spectator, but that the subject-actor appears as that gap through which the character relates to itself, "representing itself."

We have a great example of this in one of the best film comedies ever made, Ernst Lubitsch's *To Be or Not to Be*. At the beginning of the film, there is a brilliant scene in which a group of actors are rehearsing a play featuring Hitler. The director is complaining about the appearance of the actor who plays Hitler, insisting that his make-up is bad, and that he does not look like Hitler at all. He also says that what he sees in front of him is just an ordinary man. Reacting to this, one of the actors replies that Hitler *is* just an ordinary man. If this were all, we would be dealing with the logic of revealing "fundamental truths," which remains stuck halfway in relation to the properly comic way of transmitting truths. So, the scene continues: the director is still not satisfied, and tries desperately to name the mysterious "something more" that distinguishes the appearance of Hitler from the appearance of the actor in front of him. He searches around, finally sees a picture (a photograph) of Hitler on the wall, and triumphantly cries out: "That's it! That's what Hitler looks like!" "But sir," replies the actor, "that's a picture of me." This, on the contrary, is really comical. The mysterious charisma of Hitler, the thing in Hitler more than a man-named-Hitler, emerges before us as the minimal difference between the actor who plays, represents, Hitler and the photograph of this same actor. In other words, the fact that the universal of representation is related to itself produces the very concreteness of the represented. In the form of a gag, this same procedure already appears immediately before the scene just described, in a rehearsal of the same play. We are in Gestapo headquarters, and somebody announces Hitler. The doors open, and everybody raises their hands with the salute "Heil Hitler." Hitler walks in, raises his hand, and says, "Heil myself!"

It is precisely this relating of the "universal essences" (characters) to themselves and to other "universal essences" (the relating that always succeeds either too much or not enough—this is the surplus with which most comic situations and dialogues are built) that creates the movement in which the universal becomes concrete, and becomes the subject. "Stereotypical" characters as abstract universalities are set in motion and, through different accidents and events, the concrete, subjective universality is condensed or produced—the universal as subject, so convincing and powerful in good comedies. Just think of Chaplin's character, the Tramp. As such (or "in itself") this character is perfectly stereotypical and has been seen hundreds of times (if nowhere else, in Chaplin's own numerous silent comedies). Yet at the same time it would be hard to find something more concrete, subjective, and universal in the same gesture as precisely the Tramp. But not only the Tramp. Think of *The Gold Rush* or *Modern Times*—in both cases Chaplin appears with a generic name: "Lone Prospector" in the first, "Worker" in the second. We thus start with an abstract universality, which is not so much "represented" by Chaplin as forced to rise/descend to the concrete universality of the individual we see on the screen. "The Tramp," "Lone Prospector," and "Worker" are, in comedy, the very movement of becoming "trampship," "prospectorship," "workership"—that is to say, (their) subject. If we think about it for a moment, we can see how in tragedy we are in fact dealing with an opposite motion: we always start with a very concrete and strong personality, a significant individual with a proper name that often gives the tragedy its title. It would be hard to imagine, as titles of tragedies, universal or generic names—to change, for example, the title *Antigone* into *The (Untamed) Shrew*, *Othello* into *The Jealous Husband*, *Romeo and Juliet* perhaps straight into *Love's Labour's Lost*. It would indeed be hard to do this and still remain on the territory of tragedy. This, of course, is no coincidence: the two dramatic practices involve opposite motions. In tragedy the acting subject, via the various ordeals that befall her, has to let—often at the price of her own death—some universal idea, principle, or destiny shine through her. In comedy, in contrast, some universality ("tramp," "worker," "misanthrope". . .) has to let a subject in all his concreteness shine through it—not as the opposite of this universal (or as its irreducible support), but as its own inherent truth, its flexibility and life.[3]

This is why, for Hegel, comedy is not simply a turn from the universal (from universal values of the beautiful, the just, the good, the moral . . .) towards the individual or the particular (as always and necessarily imperfect, limited and always slightly idiotic), but corresponds instead to the very speculative passage from the abstract universal to the concrete universal. For Hegel, it is the abstract universal itself that is, by definition, imperfect and limited, because it lacks the moment of self-consciousness, of the self, of the concrete; it is universal and pure only at the price of being ultimately empty. The turn or shift at stake here is thus not a shift from the universal to something else, but a shift within the universal itself. The turn towards the individual is the turn of the universal itself, it is the risk and the trial of the universal. It is only as a concrete self that the universal comes to its own truth via the gap of self-consciousness. The concrete is not some unavoidable deformation of the universal, some often idiotic incorporation of an otherwise impeccable universal "spiritual" Idea or Concept, but the touchstone of Spirit itself. This is to say—and to put it bluntly—that the universal itself is precisely as idiotic as its concrete and individual appearance. The universal that does not go through this process is not a true universal, but a mere general abstraction from the concrete. It is only with the concrete that we come to the real spirit of the universal, and we could say that the materialism of comedy is precisely the materialism of the spirit. (Linguistically, we are very well aware of this: language recognizes that comedy, precisely in its materialism, is a matter of spirit; this is evident in numerous terms that link the comic mode with spirit—in the broad sense of mental capacity. Let me mention just a few: wit in English;[4] geistvoll or geistreich in German, as well as witzig and Witz, which have the common root with the English wit; French is especially eloquent in this regard—avoir de l'esprit, être spirituel, faire de l'esprit, mot d'esprit, or just simply esprit.)

With this attested affinity between spirit and comedy, it comes perhaps as no surprise that comedy ranks high in the "phenomenology of spirit." And not just because of the term spirit—could we not say that the entire movement of the *Phenomenology of Spirit* is surprisingly akin to the comic movement as described by Hegel: different figures of consciousness which follow one upon the other in this gigantic philosophical theater go, one after another, through a twist in the process by which a concrete universal is being produced and self-consciousness constituted—that is, in which substance becomes a subject. No wonder, then, that a good many of the chapter titles in *Phenomenology of Spirit* read as perfect comedy titles: "Lord and Bondsman," "The Unhappy Consciousness," "Pleasure and Necessity," "The Law of the Heart and the Frenzy of Self-Conceit," "Absolute Freedom and Terror," "Dissemblance or Duplicity," "The Beautiful Soul"—not to mention the ultimate comedy (and this is not meant ironically!) bearing the title "Absolute Knowledge."

So it is not surprising that Lacan described Hegel's *Phenomenology* as un humour fou, a crazy humor (Lacan 1991, p. 197). This humor of Hegel's might strike us as especially crazy at the point where he works out and establishes a direct passage from comedy to the very core of Christianity (as revealed religion), which he discusses in the subsequent section, focusing particularly on the moment of the Incarnation. The Essence descends from heaven to earth, and is incarnated in the concrete. It is incarnated, not represented: it is not that the transcendent, eternal Essence gets represented in this world in some concrete, finite form. When it appears in this world in a concrete form, it literally disappears from the other world, and with it disappears this other world itself. This is the famous point of the Hegelian reading of the speculative dimension of Christianity: revelation and incarnation also imply that with Christ's death on the Cross (that is, the death of the self or the subject that incarnates the Essence) it is the transcendent God himself who dies, the Beyond as such. The death of

Christ, which Hegel reads as an intrinsic moment of the Resurrection, does not mean that after it the Essence, untouched in itself, returns to the Beyond and reestablishes the latter. For this would imply that we have remained stuck with the representative logic of Greek gods as universal powers that are not limited by their own individual appearance; it would mean that we did not get past the ("bad") universality, the limit of which lies precisely in the fact that it is not limited by its own concrete individuality. Thus, the death of Christ is first and foremost the death of God as the Beyond, and the implication of this Beyond in the concrete reality of human subjects. The first moment of the Incarnation—that is to say, the Incarnation itself—posits the equation "God is man" (which is not simply reversible, and is not the same as "man is God");[5] as for the death of this Incarnation, it implies two essential points: the real death of the Beyond, and the ultimate reaffirmation of the equation "God is man." This, to be sure, is not simply an elimination of all transcendence but, rather, the affirmation of its existence as real, and always concrete.

To return to the previous point: at a time when, thanks to Mel Gibson, everybody has been talking about the Passion of the Christ, his unimaginable suffering, it would perhaps be the right moment to lend an ear to the story of the "comedy of Christ."

PHYSICS OF THE INFINITE AGAINST
METAPHYSICS OF THE FINITE

In a rather curious and intriguing paper published in 1965 by Nathan A. Scott, we find a thesis that explicitly links the Christian premise of Incarnation with comedy (and its materialism). Scott's argument is worth a brief discussion—perhaps not so much for itself as for the strategic value it can have in the context of our theme: it poses the question of materialism and comedy in an interestingly surprising way, and can help us to specify what distinguishes our argument about the materialism of comedy from a more general "humanist" one, ultimately adopted by Scott.

The first part of Scott's argument is a sort of gigantic slap in the face of modern literature. Its interest lies in the fact that the objection this Christian author raises against modern literature is none other than: modern literature is not materialistic enough; it is all too spiritualistic, it nurtures a strong belief in the transcendent and unattainable character of the Essential, and cannot stand the concreteness and contingency of human existence, which fill it with weariness and nausea. Gnosticism is the religion most fitting to "modern sensibility," and (more or less) clearly discernible in modern literature. It posits a menacing Emptiness at the center of the world, a world that has been emptied of radical significance, the world as a form of nightmare. This modern sensibility is based on the postulate of an absolute seclusion of that which is radically Significant from all the provisional and proximate meanings of historical experience, and conceives of the world of finite existence as a delusive and fraudulent imposture. There is a feeling of the radical transcendence of that which could be really Significant or Essential, and of the painful incapacity of Being ever to be able to attain it.

Woolf (The Voyage Out) and Sartre (La nausée) provide the perfect justifications for Scott's thesis. To give the reader a taste of his argumentation, this is how he describes Sartre's hero Roquentin from La nausée. Roquentin experiences a profound disgust, and is sickened "by the amorphous factuality of the phenomenal world, by the obscene stubbornness with which things persist in retaining a thereness that seems to have no link with his own existence and that seems, therefore, to that extent to oppose his own inward being." Every object and every event that he experiences "seem, in their sheer arbitrariness and contingency of their reality, to imply that the kind of metaphysical order that he craves is an impossibility. So his sense of justice is outraged, and, in his consuming disgust, he desired to be disembodied into the purity of sound made by a blues-saxophonist: he would live the incorporeal life of the angels, being no longer a man but a breath of music" (Scott 1965, p. 100). Similarly, Scott describes Woolf's specific intelligence as "an intelligence that cannot dive into the thick, coarse realities of the human condition, for these are not realities that are regarded as leading anywhere or as associable with what is Really Significant in life. There is no deep faith or confidence in the realm of human finitude," and there is "so much impatience with the clumsy grossness of the human creature and with rough, ragged edges of life . . ." (ibid., p. 99).

From these and other examples Scott deduces no less than a fundamental idealism and a specific religiosity or spirituality of modern literature, an extreme impatience with our life and our existence in time, a fundamental mistrust of the created orders of finitude. Existence in time is itself a burden, and the reality of our life is seen as shut off from the dimension of the True (significance) and the Real, submerged in the sheer banality of being. We are entrapped in this existence as in a prison cage, and our (ordinary, everyday) life is precisely that which separates us from Life in the emphatic sense of the word. In this perspective, "modern sensibility" is thus riven by a radical split between life and the "other scene," the scene of Truth and of the Really Significant, from which we are painfully secluded and which we can approach—if at all—only in a few exceptional and extreme moments of sheer intensity.

This kind of intensity, this kind of spirituality, of disembodiment, of disgust towards the existing "stupid" and meaningless Being are, according to Scott, the very opposite of the comic spirit, which thrives, and is totally submerged, in the finitude of human existence and in its materiality. The comic way descends into the mundane, conditioned world of the human creature, "moving confidently into all diverse corners of man's habitation." Hence—the eternal example!—"the humiliation that the arrogant millionaire suffers when, as he walks down the street, with his mind concentrated on his dignity and importance, he slips on the banana peeling that he failed to notice and is thus reminded that . . . he is as much subject to the law of gravitation as the rest of humankind" (Scott 1965, p. 103). Yet the comic man is unembarrassed by even the grossest expressions of his creatureliness: although the world may not be all fine and dandy, he has no sense of being under any cruel condemnation; nor does he have any sense of desperate entrapment behind prison bars. . . .

Here the other surprising tenor of Scott's argument begins: in its restoration of our confidence in the realm of finitude, comedy is governed by the same "gross materialism" as Christianity. The element of Christianity that Scott puts most emphasis on in this respect is the element of Incarnation, which he reads—at least up to certain point—in a very Hegelian way. He takes the doctrine of Incarnation to be the "heart of the Gospel," and insists very strongly upon the fact that "Jesus Christ is God Himself incarnate" (Scott 1965, p. 110). In other words, what is at stake is not merely that, through the life of Jesus the carpenter of Galilee, we might come to discern what God is like. Christ is not merely a religious genius, or a hero of some sort. Nor are we dealing with a God who, like the gods of pagan Greece, merely disguised himself as a man. Christ is God, God as man, as incarnated and existing in the human condition. It is this aspect of the Incarnation that also lies at the very heart of comedy.

With reference to Scott's own example, I am tempted to sum up his argument in the following way: Jesus Christ is the God that has slipped on the banana peel. Incarnation is comedy, and comedy always involves incarnation. How, then?! Christianity as the fight against idealism? Christianity as the struggle against the belief that we are essentially something more than finite, contingent beings? A rather startling point, one must admit, coming from a Christian author.

Yet, besides this intriguing and powerful point, there is another aspect of Scott's argument which remains "Christian" in a much more traditional way, and does not so much reveal as obfuscate some crucial dimension of comedy. For it situates comedy in a much too simplistic perspective, that of accepting the "burden" of human finitude, its limitations and embarrassments, and finding some joy in it. This point is worth addressing, because it has its revival (without its explicitly Christian surroundings) in much that has recently been said and written about comedy. It is from this perspective, for example, that comic characters are often opposed to tragic heroes and heroines, who are considered as "extremists" seeking to transcend the limitations that attach to our creatureliness,[6] and consequently forget that they are only human.

In this perspective, comedy (as the opposite of this tendency) falls back to its most boring and reductive definition: comedy is about accepting the fact that we are only human, with all the flaws and weaknesses that this implies; it helps us to recognize that beauty lies in small, banal, and everyday things (not in unattainable ideals), and—as Scott puts it—"when we wish to be pure discarnate spirit or pure discarnate intellect, the comedian asks us to remember the objective, material conditions of life with which we must make our peace, if we are to retain our sanity and survive. He will not let us forget that we are men, that we are finite and conditioned creatures—not angels" (Scott 1965, p. 113).

The definition of comedy that follows from this kind of remark is both simplistic and ideologically problematic. It is simplistic because it completely fails to see not only that comic characters are often quite "extremist" in themselves, but also that comedy always moves in both directions: not only from pure discarnate spirit to its material, physical conditions, but also from the material to forms of pure discarnate intellect, wandering around quite independently. The latter can be, and surely is, as comical as the former.

The reason for which comedy is, indeed, profoundly materialistic is not simply that it reminds us of, and insists upon, the mud, the dirt, dense and coarse reality as our ultimate horizon (which we need to accept), and as a condition of our life. Comedy is materialistic because it gives voice and body to the impasses and contradictions of this materiality itself. This is the true incarnation involved in comedy. The body is not the limit of a "pure intellect" seeking to be independent, but the very point of its origin. If the materiality of the body is what stops things from going beyond a certain limit, it is also what sets these things in motion to begin with. Comedy is materialistic because it knows this, not because it counterbalances idealistic escapades with the limitations posed by dense material reality. The fascination with everything that is coarse and dense can be a way of avoiding a crucial lesson of materialism, which refers to the inconsistencies and contradictions of matter itself. Comedy is materialistic because it sees the turning of materiality into pure spirit and of pure spirit into something material as *one and the same movement*, driven by a difficulty inherent to materiality itself.

Some of Scott's conclusions concerning the genre of comedy, sketched out above, lead more or less directly to a point that is being all but constantly made, repeated, reaffirmed in the modern (and postmodern, or let us simply say post-Hegelian) discussion of comedy, a point which also situates this genre in a wider philosophical, political, and ideological context. This point, which I would like to challenge in this chapter, has various different formulations, which can be summed up as follows. Comedy is a genre that strongly emphasizes our essential humanity, its joys and limitations. It invites—or even forces—us to recognize and accept the fact that we are finite beings. It teaches us that we are *only human*, with all our faults, imperfections, and weaknesses, and it helps us to deal affirmatively and joyfully with the burden of human finitude.

It is rather amazing how these "modern" views on comedy are irresistibly driven towards pathos (an affect which is, in fact, as far as possible from the true comic spirit), and how comedy's supposed celebration of human finitude often seems to be the principal argument when it comes to justifying serious theoretical or philosophical attention to this traditionally rather underrated genre. And if modern readers are often taken aback by Hegel's discussing comedy (and art) in the context of religion, they seem to have fewer problems embracing this kind of discussion, which can hardly be said to be any less overdetermined by a very similar set of questions.

For quite some time, a lot of critical philosophical work has been dedicated to various ways of undermining the metaphysics of infinity, and of transcendence. Yet we should not overlook the fact that there is also a considerable (modern) corpus of what I would call a *metaphysics of finitude* in which, often with a distinctively pathetic ring to it, finitude appears as *our* (contemporary) great narrative. The range of this metaphysics of finitude is considerable; it stretches from very complex and highly elaborate philosophical enterprises to an utterly commonsense "psycho-theology of everyday life" (to borrow, with different signifying implications, Eric Santner's expression), in which finitude appears as consolation for, and explanation of, our little (or not so little) disappointments and misfortunes, as a new Master-Signifier summoned to make sense of our ("acknowledged") senseless existence, as a new Gospel or "good news": You're only human! Give yourself a break! Nobody's perfect!

Those who recall the famous last scene from Billy Wilder's *Some Like It Hot* (the last sentence of the movie is precisely "Nobody's perfect") know how spectacularly, and at the same time most precisely, comedy can subvert this great wisdom (which is even supposed to be the wisdom of comedy): nobody's perfect, therefore it doesn't matter what you say or do, or what you are; you'd better shut up and let us do exactly what we want to do with you (for instance: marry you, as the gag goes in the movie). Or, as this wisdom concerning human (im)perfection is turned around in another comic twist: "Nobody's perfect. I am nobody."

The prizing of comedy as a *porte-parole* of human finitude (and of everything that is supposed to be related to it: acceptance of our weaknesses, limitations, and imperfections; reconciliation with the absence of the transcendent and acknowledgment of the equation "a human is [only] human," "life is [only] life") is conceptually highly problematic. Such a perspective on comedy is much too simplistic, and soon turns out to be pretty useless. Is it not, rather, that the exact opposite rings truer? If humans were "only human(s)" (and life "only life"), if the human equation indeed added up so neatly and with no remainder, *there would be no comedy.* Is not the very existence of comedy and of the comical telling us most clearly that a man is never just a man, and that his finitude is very much corroded by a passion which is precisely not cut to the measure of man and of his finitude? Most comedies set up a configuration in which one or several characters depart violently from the moderate, balanced rationality and normality of their surroundings, and of other people in it. And, if anything, it is precisely these other, "normal" people who are "only human" or "only men," whereas this is far from being the case with comic characters. There is something very real in comedy's supposedly unrealistic insistence on the indestructible, on something that persists, keeps reasserting itself and won't go away, like a tic that goes on even though its "owner" is already dead. In this respect, one could say that the flaws, extravagances, excesses, and so-called human weaknesses of comic characters are precisely what account for their *not* being "only human." More precisely, they show us that what is "human" exists only in this kind of excess over itself.

Thus, although it is true that comedy incites a certain good-humored attitude towards human "weaknesses," the important additional emphasis is that these weaknesses are precisely something on account of which a man is never only a man. We are not merely playing with words here, reversing their meaning. What is at stake is a point that is essential for the understanding of comedy: "man," a human being, interests comedy at the very point where the human coincides with the inhuman; where the inhuman "falls" into the human (into man), where the infinite falls into the finite, where the Essence falls into appearance and the Necessary into the contingent. And if it is true that the comic universe—much more than the tragic universe—builds within the horizon of immanence, that it abandons the reference to the Beyond and always situates the Essence in a concretely existing situation, it does not do so simply by closing off its finite self in relation to the (infinite) Beyond, by excluding it from its field of reference. On the contrary, it does so by including it in the immanence, in the given situation. The Beyond is included in the world and in the human as the heterogeneous element on account of which a man is never simply and only a man. "Man is only man" is ultimately an axiom of abstract idealism; basically, it states nothing but "man is not God." Whereas the true materialistic axiom, promoted by comedy, is, rather, "a man is not a man." This is what the above-mentioned metaphysics of finitude fails to see when it encloses itself within a heart-stirring humanism of accepting human weaknesses and flaws.

To sum up: there is a significant attempt to think comedy through the notion of finitude (that is to say, of its acknowledgment and acceptance) and to promote comedy as the *porte-parole* of the contemporary metaphysics of finitude. Against this, we should insist that the true comic spirit, far from being reducible to this metaphysics of the finite, is, rather, always a "physics of the infinite." Moreover, it is precisely this physics of the infinite that situates comedy on the ground of true materialism, exempts it from all forms of spiritualism, and also gives it its contrareligious thrust—not in any simple sense of static opposition, or of mocking the infinite Other, but, rather, by deploying this infinite Other as the very material Real of human life as such.

This is also a point, I believe, where the Hegelian and the Lacanian perspectives meet, although they start from rather different perspectives. For how does the Lacanian perspective differ from the contemporary doxa of human finitude? Certainly not by nurturing a belief in immortality, nor by maintaining that there is a part or a dimension of men—call it the soul or the subject (as opposed to the individual or the ego)—which is as such infinite. The difference is much more interesting. The predominant contemporary concept of human finitude is, of course, also not simply that of reminding us that sooner or later we will drop dead, and no soul will leave our body to join its heavenly Father. It refers—to put it simply—to limits and limitations of living human beings. Here finitude is but the emphatic notion, a Master-Signifier of all that human life implies in terms of limitations, incompleteness, division, out-of-jointness, antagonism, exposure to others, "castration"; of impasses of desire, of two or more ends that never exactly coincide to form a perfect circle. It is about a chiasm that fundamentally determines the human condition. It is not also, however, that in this discourse, in the way it uses finitude as its Master-Signifier, the latter appears precisely as the closure of that which is said to resist any closure? This is most clearly detectible precisely in the redoubling of a description by prescription, in the passage from "We are limited, divided, exposed beings" to "Be limited, divided, exposed!" (that is to say, you must accept this)—whereby the latter constitutes the ethical part of contemporary thought concerning human finitude. We can see here a kind of reversal of Wittgenstein and his "Whereof one cannot speak, thereon one must remain silent"; it is not a paradoxical prohibition of the impossible but, rather, a paradoxical injunction of the possible, of what there is. Despite numerous references, in this ethics, to the possibility of change and of emancipatory politics, this possibility is largely blocked precisely by the imperative of the possible. In relation to this, the Lacanian stance is not—as it is sometimes described, or criticized—that of an imperative of the impossible, of forcing oneself (or others) beyond the limits of what is humanly possible. As I have argued elsewhere in more detail,[7] the point of Lacan's identification of the Real with the impossible is not that the Real is some Thing that cannot possibly happen—the whole point of the Lacanian concept of the Real is that the impossible happens.

Already desire in its radical negativity—but especially the drive, with its always excessive, "surplus" nature—necessarily complicate the story of accepting one's finitude, since they introduce (or point to) a fundamental *contradiction in this finitude itself*. One could, of course, retort that this human contradiction is the very mark of its finitude. Yet this move is precisely that of closure. Instead, one should take a conceptual step further: It is not simply that, as human beings, we are marked by a fundamental contradiction and are therefore finite—contradiction applies, or extends, to this very finitude as our "human condition." For what is at stake could be formulated as follows: our finitude is always-already a *failed finitude*—one could say a finitude with a leak in it. Lacan situates the "leak" in the point of incidence of the signifier. The nature of this incidence is always problematic; the link between the body and the signifier produces and includes a point that is not reducible to either one of them. To put it very simply: in order for this link to be established, something needs to be subtracted (from the body). This produces a third element, a blueprint of a third dimension of human existence, which is not simply the body, and does not have a symbolic standing: Lacan calls it the "partial object," the object *a*. Object *a* is the Lacanian name for the materiality of the leak in human finitude. It is the very thing that runs against and belies the doxa that "there are only bodies and languages" (to borrow Badiou's definition of "democratic materialism").[8]

It is precisely this "failed finitude," especially in its object form, that comedy thrives on. The conceptual point—deployed, in a theatrical way, by comedy—is none other than this: the finitude of human reality is, at the very outset, a paradoxical finitude, a finitude with a flaw. For human beings there is no such thing as an unproblematic finitude (which, for some mysterious reason, they would refuse to accept). Would it not be more correct to say that humankind would be more than happy to be able to live peacefully in its finitude, but that there is something that gnaws away at this finitude from within, erodes it, puts it into question? This situation is excellently defined by one of Beckett's interpreters, who describes Beckett's hero in this way: "À défaut d'être immortel, il est increvable!"—He may not be immortal, but he's *indestructible!*" (Simon 1963, p. 130).[9]

Human finitude has a hole in it, and it is precisely this "hole" (and its consequences) that different religious discourses both mobilize as their driving force and respond to by their narratives, which provide specific frames of reference for this failed finitude. In this respect, if atheism means anything, it means that the one thing "modern" man needs to accept or take upon himself is not (simply) finitude, but precisely this "hole in finitude," instead of hopelessly and always unsuccessfully "filling it in" with more or less pathetic assertions about human finitude.

In this perspective, the most accurate way to articulate the question of human finitude/infinitude would be to say: *Not only are we not infinite, we are not even finite.*

If we stop here and think again about comedy, we can perhaps see more clearly that the stuff that comedies are made of is precisely this hole in finitude, in its different and various forms. Comic characters, as well as comic situations, do not only expose this fact, but also use it abundantly as the very generative source of what they themselves create and play with. This is what the chapters that follow will try to show more in detail and more concretely.

One last remark should be added here as a conclusion to this discussion of finitude, concerning the notion of internal contradiction as opposed to that of an Other scene/world. To put it simply: the "something in life more (or less) than life" can be seen either as a sublime phenomenal manifestation of the Other scene, or as a real creation or product of life's own inherent contradiction ("nonwholeness"). The first alternative is obviously that of transcendence, with all its theological implications. We are human, and as such finite, but at the same time we participate in something bigger: in the infinite Other that also beholds our truth, which cannot be reduced to the empirical description of our lives.

The perspective of inherent contradiction (there is no Other side; what looks like the Other side is an inherent contradiction of one and the same side) is by no means simple. It is not simply about immanence, but involves an immanent transcendence. To articulate it, Lacan had recourse to topology and came up with the figure of the Möbius strip.

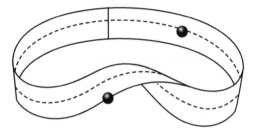

Perhaps the simplest way of describing the Möbius strip would be to say that it has, at every point, two sides (the surface and its other side), yet *there is only one surface*. Starting at any point on the strip and continuing the movement along the same side, without ever crossing the edge, we come sooner or later to the reverse side of the point where we started. Or, as Lacan puts it: an insect walking on this surface can believe at every moment that there is a side which it hasn't explored, the other side of that on which it walks. It can strongly believe in this other side, in this beyond, even though there is no other side, as we know. Without knowing this, the insect thus explores the only side there is (Lacan 2004, p. 161). The paradox embodied by the topology of the Möbius strip thus consists in there being only one surface (in this sense we are dealing with immanence), yet at every point there is also the other side. It is in this sense that we should understand the concept of inherent contradiction (of the finite) as the generating point of something that is not reducible to simple finitude.

Yet this perspective of internal contradiction can itself have quite different destinies and articulations. I call metaphysics of the finite the destiny/articulation that, basically, always follows the structure of "bad infinity." It is satisfied by pointing out not an finite, but an *endless* movement of contradiction, and responds to it by a never-ending process of differentiation.

Then there is the subjectivation—or, perhaps better, an individualization—of this endless movement of contradiction, which could be recognized as the essence of tragedy or of the "tragic paradigm" (one could also say of the heroic paradigm). By choice or by play of circumstances, the tragic hero comes to embody and to be the playground of this endless contradiction, which cannot but tear him or her apart, destroy him or her (as an individual). This involves a certain gesture of totalization: at the price of her "material" destruction, the subject represents the nonrepresentable, "infinite" whole, which in turn becomes (is elevated into) a subjective figure, and is visible as such. This is the kind of totalization that Kant discusses in his theory of the sublime: that of encompassing an endless series in one intuition, whereby representation succeeds by its very failure.

And then there is also a possible "objectification" (or singularization) of the (endless) internal contradiction, which one could relate, among other things, to comedy and to the "comic paradigm." The logic here is not that of encompassing a possible endless series in which contradiction is played out but, rather, that of singularizing it, objectifying the contradiction itself. This is the incarnation proper, as different from (tragic, or other) embodiment. If the movement of inherent contradiction keeps producing two heterogeneous sides of human experience, irreducible to one another, there is a difference between the embodiment ("personification") of this split on the one hand, and its incarnation on the other. Comic incarnation is a surprising short circuit between the two sides. With the topology of the Möbius strip in mind, we could say that, fundamentally, comic procedure is a procedure designed to make us see the impossible passage from one side to the other, or the impossible link between the two.

If we are to understand this correctly, we must be careful not to understand the term "missing link" too hastily. The value of the topological model of the Möbius strip lies in the fact that the structural or constitutive missing link is precisely not something that one could see as a missing link or a lack. After all, the Möbius strip presents us with nothing more than a smooth continuity of the same surface, with no interruptions, lacks, or leaps. The leap, the paradoxical distance between its two sides, is "built into" its very structure; it is perceptible only in the fact that we do come to change sides, even though we never actually change them. In other words, the whole point of the Möbius strip is to help us think a singular kind of missing link: not a link that is missing from a chain (which would be thus interrupted), but a link which is missing in a way that enables the very linking of the existing elements, their being bound, attached to one another, their forming a chain, a smooth (causal) sequence. The missing nature of this link is never visible, perceptible, but is implicated in the way the chain is ("positively") formed, what elements it links together and at what points; it is not a missing link between two neighbor elements, the connection between which would thus be interrupted—instead, its very missing is the linkage between two neighbor elements, it is what makes it possible for them to fit into each other, so to speak.

There are two fundamental comic procedures which somehow make this singular kind of missing link appear. One is the sudden intrusion of the other side, followed by an "impossible articulation" of the two sides in one and the same frame. A good example of this procedure is an excellent (English) comic sketch, designed as publicity for a mobile phone company. The general situation is a (stereo)typical situation of adultery. A man comes home from work earlier than usual, and finds his wife in bed. She is visibly upset by his arrival, and claims to be in bed because she has a terrible headache. While he is expressing his concern for her, a phone starts to ring. The man reaches for his phone and answers, but the ringing continues. He is perplexed, and keeps looking at the phone in his hand; then the door of the bedroom closet opens and another man, wearing only his socks, comes out. He apologizes for the inconvenience and heads for the heap of clothes lying in the corner of the room, in search of the phone, which continues to ring. He finds it, answers it, and gets very seriously engaged in conversation. Meanwhile he is gesticulating to the (staring) husband and wife, to express his regret at intruding on them with his phone conversation. As if to minimize this impolite intrusion, he moves back towards the closet, climbs in, closes the door behind him, and calmly continues his conversation inside. . . .

There are, of course, many details that make this scene funny, but there is also something in its very structure that is irresistibly comical: precisely the impossible sustained encounter between two excluding realities. Comedy stages this encounter in its very impossibility. In "ordinary reality" this kind of intrusion of the other side would cause an immediate reaction and adjustment of both sides, enabling the linear continuation of the story. The lover would be embarrassed, the husband humiliated, the wife embarrassed and perhaps scared; there would be a confrontation—that is to say, some kind of acknowledgment of what happened, and of its necessary consequences. In our comic example, however, it is precisely this acknowledgment that is suspended, enabling the two mutually exclusive realities to continue to exist alongside each other, and, moreover, to be articulated within one and the same scene. The actual link between them, the way the two realities meet and are articulated together (the lover politely apologizing to the couple for the disturbance caused by his phone, and considerately retreating back to his closet so that he does not disturb them with his talking) is, of course, highly illogical and "fantastic," yet it works. In other words, it is not only that this comic procedure presents us with two mutually exclusive realities as visible in one and the same "shot," it also has to find and offer us a form of their articulation which, in all its "absurdity," somehow works.

The linkage must not be simply and utterly absurd. More precisely, the absurd is the very limit of comedy, and may already function as comedy, yet the more it moves towards some form of "nonsense that nevertheless makes sense," the more intense its comic effect becomes. This "illogical, yet logical" linkage is the very positive form in which appears the constitutively missing link which—in the very fact that it is missing—provides the apparent coherence of a given linear reality.

We should thus be careful not to reduce the comedy of this scene simply to its protagonists deliberately ignoring what really happened, to the lover's incredible diversion from the Real of what happened. For it is not as if the lover acts as he does in a desperate attempt to avoid confrontation; his interest in his phone conversation is presented as absolutely genuine, and it "genuinely" prevails over his concern with the rest of the situation; this enables the two mutually exclusive realities to be articulated together, visible at the same time. In other words, the Real "exposed" by comedy is usually not the Real of what happened, but the structural Real (or impasse) the suppression of which constitutes the very coherence of our reality. By ignoring the Real of what happened, comedy succeeds in displaying the crack in the midst of our most familiar realities. And this is the real core of comedy. That is also to say that the *intrusion of the other side,* which is one of the most common comic procedures, is not simply about the other side undermining, even destroying, this side. Although this destruction may occur at some point, it never constitutes the heart of a comic scene. The first and the main comic purpose of the intrusion of the other side lies in what it enables in terms of juxtaposition of the two sides, their contemporaneity, their "impossible" joint articulation. This joint articulation can be very restricted and momentary, or extensively sustained, which is often the case. Yet we should not fail to see its central comic role also when it is only brief and transitory.

Another comic procedure that results in a kind of short circuit between a reality and its other side is comic acceleration or exaggeration. In relation to the image of the Möbius strip, we could describe it as a forced (yet again somehow "illogically logical") and strongly accelerated taking a few steps forward from the point on which we are standing. These few big steps bring us to the other side of our point of departure before we even realize it. This is a procedure amply used, for example, in the movie Borat: if, in the general configuration of the movie, a stuffy, sleazy, and prejudiced dump is the other side of the glorious, prosperous, politically correct Democracy, then the character of Borat is very successful in provoking his interlocutors into taking a few quick steps that lead them to the point where they no longer recognize themselves, and no longer know where they stand. We start from a certain point, and within a single shot or sequence we reach its other side, which again produces the effect of juxtaposing the two mutually exclusive points, of articulating them together. Here again, the point is not that of one side undermining the other, or of constituting the "truth" of the other. Their truth is their joint articulation, which is never visible in the given reality, yet is constitutive of it. This "impossible" joint articulation is, I would claim, the real comic object.

Both these procedures are examples of the properly comic implication of the other side within this side. And it is the very material point of this implication or inclusion that constitutes the site of the infinite that comedy never renounces. This could be further illustrated and related back to the question of the concrete universal if we briefly stop to consider the difference between irony and comedy proper. This difference is exactly the one between pointing out the limits and limitations of, for example, the universal, and endorsing these limits by transforming them into the very points of the infinite and generic power of the universal. Let us first take the famous double graffiti:

"God is dead." Nietzsche

"Nietzsche is dead." God

This is irony at its purest, in its minimal formula. The ironic turn brings out the limitation, the particular, concrete determination of the place of enunciation, which then belies the universality of the statement. The point of the ironic twist, of course, is not simply to reaffirm God against Nietzsche; the supplement it introduces is there to foreground the gap between the statement (its content, which is supposed to be universal) and the place of enunciation (which is supposed to be always particular), and this gap is used to "prove" the impossibility (the internal contradiction) of universal statements or truths. Any universal statement could be disproved by pointing to the particular (concrete) place of its enunciation. In this sense, the ironic procedure is potentially endless; it deploys the internal contradiction of reality in a series of twists performed on the given elements of reality, exposing their contradiction. Yet does not the limit of this kind of irony lie in the fact that it does not recognize the possibility of a "concrete universal" (as well as the possibility of an "abstract particularity"), and remains within the parameters of the opposition between abstract universality and concrete particularity? And is not the twist introduced by the true comic spirit precisely something that cuts across this opposition, and bets on the possibility of a concrete universal? In the context of our example, the true comic twist would thus take the following form:

"God is dead. And I'm not feeling too well either."

This is a splendid example of the "singular universality" which includes the infinite in the finite, and could be defined as follows: what is at stake is not simply the universal value of a statement (of its content), but the universalizability of the place of enunciation itself. In this case, the place of enunciation does not undermine the universality of the statement but becomes its very internal gap, that which alone generates the only (possible) universality of the statement.

PART II

FIGURES OF COMEDY

THE EGO AND THE IT

In many languages there is a splendid and constantly used form of polite question. In English the question is: *How's it going?* The greatness of this formula resides in the fact that the usual answer (*Very well, thank you*) leaves wonderfully intact the ambiguity of this question, its two possible "subjects." In order to see this, it is enough to shift the accent a little and to emphasize the "it" in "How's it going?" What I have in mind is that the full answer to the question *How's it going?* might very well be something like: It is going very well. But me—well, that's another matter. I'm tired, I'm depressed, my back aches. . . .

What comes to the foreground here is the split between—to use the famous Freudian title—*das Ich und das Es*, "the Ego and the Id," as two possible addressees of the question, as well as the fact that the "id/it" usually blindly goes its own way, paying little attention to the ego to which it is attached, so to speak. In other words: It/Id is always doing well, it finds its own ways of satisfaction, even at the expense of the subject, who has no option but to complain. In a word, this is a fine reminder that "the Ego and the Id" do not necessarily feel the same amount of happiness and content when it comes to the fortunes and misfortunes of life.

This anecdotal remark is not a bad way of embarking on a discussion of one of the crucial dimensions of the comical. There is a whole spectrum of comic situations and occurrences that one could place under the heading of "the Ego and the Id/It," and relate them to the fact that there is between the two a fundamental discrepancy, incongruence, disproportion. People have most peculiar ways of finding satisfaction. The discrepancies between what I want and what I enjoy are the bread and butter of comedies. So is the fact that something in me can be satisfied even though "I" find no satisfaction, or that the satisfaction of the "I" can be so great that it is ready to cut itself off from the interests of the body. There is not much point in enumerating all the possible situations here—let me just say that they all revolve around the fact that there is something about satisfaction and enjoyment that has its own logic and a relatively independent autonomous life, which can land the subject in rather awkward situations.

When it comes to the question of happiness and satisfaction, we automatically suppose that it is the ego that has to be happy, and that "I am happy" actually means "my I (meaning the ego) is happy." This is by no means self-evident. Indeed—and in the terms of the Freudian topography—why the ego and not, rather, the superego or the id? Or, for that matter, why not the sexual organ? In *Seminar XVII*, Jacques Lacan briefly rebukes, in a kind of comic interlude, the predominant ideological tendency of the *International Journal of Psycho-Analysis*, preoccupied, at the time, with two main themes: the theme of an autonomous ego and the theme of happiness (themes, one could say, that have since invaded every aspect of our daily life). Lacan first points out that nobody actually knows what this happiness would be, except if one takes it to mean "to be like everybody else"—which, he goes on, is precisely the meaning of the celebrated "autonomous ego": my "ego" is happy and autonomous when it is the same as everybody else's. At this point Lacan intervenes with an abrupt statement that functions as a genuine psychoanalytic gag: *there is only the happiness of the phallus*. The emphasis, he explains, is on the fact that it is only the phallus that is happy—not its bearer (Lacan 1991, p. 84). The latter may feel rather frustrated: there is something there that does not concern him, something that is annoyingly indifferent (and unrelated) to his feelings. The thing is happy, well and good, but what about him, what about the "I," what about the ego? This comic Lacanian interlude is itself based on the comedy of the parting of the ego and the Id/It.

To return to the previous discussion: the type of comic situations where a more or less agreeable image of the ego is challenged by the intrusion of some fundamental need that demands its satisfaction is very common and extends through numerous registers, from the most elementary to the very complex. How do we explain the puzzlingly infallible comic hold that this ridiculous, stupidly simple situation has on us: somebody is walking energetically, zealously down the street, then suddenly slips and falls flat on his face? Is this not, among other things, a rudimentary matrix of the ego parting company with the It? It is as if, for a brief moment, we saw the "ego" continuing to walk down the street, whereas the It was lying flat on the ground. I have already made a few comments about the properly comic articulation of two excluding realities on one scene, and we can note this same mechanism at work in this simple example: the sudden intrusion of the other reality is not funny simply because the zealous ego finally crashes flat on the street, pulled down by its own body, so to speak. It is funny because of what it produces in this movement: the very visibility of the split between the ego and the It, the very visibility of the two as separate, albeit related, entities. What we see in ordinary circumstances is a (more or less) coherent unity in which, in effect, the body is smoothly, imperceptibly passing into the ego, and the ego into the body. This is what it means to be "collected," "composed." What the sudden fall produces in place of this imaginary Unity is a short circuit between the two facets which involves a comical decomposition of the Unity, and confronts us directly with the question of the (missing) link between the two sides of the same reality that thus become visible in the same "shot"—they are visible until the person "collects" herself again. We could say that the comic short circuit is a manifestation of the missing link which, in the very fact that it is missing, holds a given reality together, whereas Unity functions as a veiling of this missing link.

This example of somebody suddenly falling flat on the street is of course not only very simple and elementary, but also very brief and momentary in displaying the nonrelation between two linked facets of reality. It is more a gag than a comedy proper, although comedy, in its burlesque version, can be "put together" by the simple means of a serial accumulation of this kind of gag. Yet if one is to distinguish between the mode of a gag and the comedy mode proper, one would have to look for the difference in the way in which comedy manages to stretch the momentariness of the short circuit, how it manages to *faire la comédie*, to "make a (whole) scene" out of this structural moment, by not simply letting it go, by insisting on it "beyond reason," and exploring it from different angles. In other words—by refusing to "cut the comedy."

A well-known comic device to ensure an extended short circuit of this kind is the invention of the Character. "Character," as invented by comedy, is something other than a "strong personality," a hero or a heroine. As Walter Benjamin has pointed out, the creation of a character does not rely upon any psychological analysis, it does not involve a person in all her "complexity," it does not seek to define a person by the multiplicity of her character traits, it is not a study that would make us understand the person's actions. Rather, the character appears in the form of its *einziger Zug*, its "single trait" (Benjamin 2004, p. 205). This single trait—or, as the term *ein einziger Zug* is usually translated in Freudian–Lacanian literature, this "unary trait"—is the essence and the form of (comic) character. In our present context, this insightful remark could be further developed. For what is a "unary trait"? It could be defined precisely as that which marks a singular coincidence or short circuit between the signifier and the body, or between subjectivity as pure lack circulating in the Symbolic, and subjectivity as a specific mode of enjoyment. Yet if, in its ordinary functioning, we get to see only its signifying facet, and can identify with it insofar as its link with the enjoyment remains veiled, invisible, secret, this is not how it appears in comedy. For the comic character could be defined precisely as an enjoying incarnation of some unary trait. It is a unary trait walking around. And it is invented for us in the form of the person's passionate attachment to a singular object or activity, that is to say, in the form of a (materially) visible tie between an Ego and its It, to use the terms of the previous discussion.

Characters (or character comedies) are indeed the prominent form taken by the figure of comedy that I have defined as that of the Ego and the It—simply because it is its singular, exclusive, and appropriately overemphasized relation to the It that makes an Ego a Character. I should add here that the term character is to be taken in its strong sense; that is to say, not all "comic characters" are characters in this sense. One could perhaps make a distinction between comic characters and comic figures. Characters are defined by the fact that they are driven utterly and exclusively by some kind of passion or passionate attachment, this passion being incarnated in an external object or ritual, which sort of "drags" these characters along, implicating them in all sorts of possible and impossible situations. This passion is out there, in the open, the comic character doesn't try to conceal or hide it (although he can stubbornly hide and protect the object of this passion—but this is another matter); that is to say, we are dealing not so much with the protagonist's "inner struggle" as with the fact that the Id—incarnated in an external object or ritual—literally swings the character around, as if they were tied together by an invisible elastic band. What first comes to mind in this respect is a whole list of Molière's characters: Harpagon—"the miser" of *The Miser*, Tartuffe (and perhaps even more his "dupe" Orgon), Don Juan, Alceste (*Misanthrope*), Arnolf (*School for Wives*), and so on. Molière was undoubtedly the great master of the construction of comic characters. (And what first comes to mind in the context of contemporary comedy is perhaps the figure of the obsessional neurotic, such as one finds in some of the better Woody Allen movies, or in Jack Nicholson's character in *As Good As It Gets*.)

An almost proverbial comic example of this kind of passionate attachment of the character is Harpagon the miser. In the famous monologue—after his treasure disappears from the garden where he has buried it—he gives vent to his passion in the following way:

HARPAGON: Alas! my poor money! my poor money! My dearest friend, they have bereaved me of thee; and since thou art gone, I have lost my support, my consolation, and my joy. All is ended for me, and I have nothing more to do in the world! Without thee it is impossible for me to live. It is all over with me; I can bear it no longer. I am dying; I am dead; I am buried. . . . I will demand justice, and have the whole of my house put to the torture—my maids and my valets, my son, my daughter, and myself too. What a crowd of people are assembled here!

Everyone seems to be my thief. . . . Quick! Magistrates, police, provosts, judges, racks, gibbets, and executioners. I will hang everybody, and if I do not find my money, I will hang myself afterwards.

(*The Miser*, Act IV, Scene VII)[1]

Even in these few extracts from a much longer monologue we can see, among other things, how a passionate attachment to an "it" that embodies all the character's passion implies, at the same time, a passionate detachment from all other institutional as well as family bonds. (And even a passionate detachment from oneself, or one's ego: Harpagon calmly includes himself in the line of suspects who must be tortured.) We find an identical structure of a paradoxical "autonomy" that the character acquires thanks to his enslavement to a certain object in the case of Orgon and his passionate belief in the hypocrite Tartuffe. This is how he prizes him:

ORGON: He is a man . . . who . . . ah! . . . in fact . . . a man.
Whoever does his will, knows perfect peace,
And counts the whole world else, as so much dung.
His converse has transformed me quite; he weans
My heart from every friendship, teaches me
To have no love for anything on earth;
And I could see my brother, children, mother,
And wife, all die, and never care—a snap.

(*Tartuffe*, Act I, Scene VI)

The Harpagons and Orgons go a step further than heroic characters who are ready to sacrifice everything for their Cause: they do not even perceive it as a sacrifice. . . .

Something else, related to this comic autonomy, is evident from these examples: characters are never "intersubjective." Although comedy, as opposed to tragedy, is above all a dialogical genre (whereas it would be difficult to have a real tragedy without a few great monologues), the type of comic characters we are discussing is fundamentally "monological." What is at stake is not merely a parody of tragic monologues, although this aspect also exists, and often plays its part in comedy. The crucial point is that these heroes are extracted, by their passion, from the world of the normal intersubjective communication—they are quite content, one could say, to converse solely with their "it/id." Yet they remain a part of this same world, which will not leave them in peace. This configuration brings about a specific comic genre of "dialogical monologue" in which the characters, technically in dialogue with others, are in fact absorbed in a dialogue with themselves, or with their "it." The comedy of such dialogues does not come from witty and clever exchanges between two subjects, or from local misunderstandings that make (comic) sense on another level of the dialogue, but from the fact that the character is not really present in the dialogue he is engaged in—or, perhaps more precisely, from the fact that he is present in it only with his "it," not as a subject. Take the following example, where Orgon, head of the family into which Tartuffe has recently forced his way, returns from a short trip and is questioning the servant Dorine about the state of his household.

(To Dorine)

ORGON: Has everything gone well these last two days?
What's happening? And how is everybody?

DORINE: Madam had fever, and a splitting headache
Day before yesterday, all day and evening.

ORGON: And how about Tartuffe?

DORINE: Tartuffe? He's well;
He's mighty well; stout, fat, fair, rosy-lipped.

ORGON: Poor man!

DORINE: At evening she had nausea
And couldn't touch a single thing for supper,
Her headache still was so severe.

ORGON: And how
About Tartuffe?

DORINE: He supped alone, before her,
And unctuously ate up two partridges,
As well as half a leg o' mutton, deviled.

ORGON: Poor man!

DORINE: All night she couldn't get a wink
Of sleep, the fever racked her so; and we
Had to sit up with her till daylight.

ORGON: How
About Tartuffe?

DORINE: Gently inclined to slumber,
He left the table, went into his room,
Got himself straight into a good warm bed,
And slept quite undisturbed until next morning.

ORGON: Poor man!

DORINE: At last she let us all persuade her,
And got up courage to be bled; and then
She was relieved at once.

ORGON: And how about
Tartuffe?

DORINE: He plucked up courage properly,
Bravely entrenched his soul against all evils,
And to replace the blood that she had lost,
He drank at breakfast four huge draughts of wine.

ORGON: Poor man!

(*Tartuffe*, Act I, Scene V)

The comedy of this dialogue does not spring simply from its content—that is, from Orgon's absolute lack of interest in "Madam's"—his wife's—health, contrasted with his infatuation with Tartuffe. What gives this "dialogue" its comic thrust lies much more in its specific form, the fact that it is actually a double monologue, or a dialogue in which the two protagonists hold their monologues through each other. Orgon is interested in only one thing, and Dorine wants to tell him only about the other thing. In his rapture, Orgon is literally out of step with the rest of the world. He blindly and stubbornly follows his "it," and Dorine tries to draw his attention to something else. With this dragging and pushing in the other direction, she creates the conditions for a visible and ongoing stretching of the tie between (Orgon's) "ego" and the "id," which is one of the essential elements in this kind of comedy.

Moreover, we should not fail to see how this double monologue in the form of a dialogue is yet another example of the comic procedure of combining, in one scene, two different, incompatible realities. It functions as a sustained "impossible" (and thus "funny") articulation of two elements that cannot be articulated together.

A further trait of this comic configuration of the Ego and the It, as illustrated in the form of Character, is a specific relationship of this Character to the issue of happiness. Since happiness is an important matter in comedy—and we will have the opportunity to discuss this below—it is worth pointing out that Characters (in the strong sense of the word) can be individuals who are not particularly happy: they are often paranoid, miserable, even bitter, constantly worried about their It, unable to trust anyone. Yet this specific paranoid or overprotective passion in relation to their object reveals a more interesting configuration: the other side of the misery of the character's Ego is the happiness of his It. In other words—and here we come back to Lacan's humorous remark— in the case of this group of comic characters we can clearly see that, for example, the happiness of the phallus is to be distinguished from the happiness of its bearer. Or, to put it more generally, we can see that it is only their It that is happy. "They," on the other hand, do everything and go to great lengths to make and keep the It as happy as possible; this can indeed put them in stressful and often miserable positions. However, we should go a step further here and recognize that they do not really mind this misery at all. They might constantly complain, yet this does not indicate that they are not satisfied with things as they are. They do not feel unhappy because they are miserable and in a constant state of stress. On the contrary: they are quite content insofar as their It is content, and insofar as they manage to keep it content.

THE EGO AND THE EGO

The next structural theme, so to speak, which thrives in comedy is the theme of the double. In its elementary form—that is to say, before it grows into all possible variations of redoubling and of confused identities—this theme is actually nothing but the introduction of the Ego/I into what is called objective reality. One of the earliest discoveries revealed by comedy is that the ego (the "I") is an object (that is, an object among others in the world of objects), that "egos exist"—and, of course, that the ego is in itself an eminently comical character. Yet the ego had first to walk onto the stage—not simply as the ego of this or that person, his or her "psychological center," but as the ego *tout court*. And this happened in around 200 BC, when Plautus wrote *Amphitryon*, one of the greatest paradigmatic comedies, which served as a model for a whole series of further variations (reportedly almost forty), the most famous of which is probably Molière's. The comedy of this comedy starts with the following epochal retort:

MERCURY: Who goes there?
SOSIE: I.

Sosie, to be sure, is not simply someone who says "I"; something else, and more, is at stake: Sosie has made it into the French dictionary: *sosie* has become the name of the "I," the name of the ego or, more precisely, the name of the ego that one comes across in external reality, that is, the name of the other ego, the *alter ego*, the double. We should perhaps point out the slight difference between the French original and the English translation, on account of which the French text opens with the question of the Ego even more explicitly. In compliance with French grammar, Sosie's reply to Mercury's question is *moi* (not *je*—although, later on, the ambiguity of *je* also gets to play its part). In French these opening lines thus imply something very close to: *Who goes there?—Ego.*

Let us first briefly recall the story of *Amphitryon*. The god Jupiter has a very worldly crush on Amphitryon's wife, Alcmena, whom he wants to seduce. Since Alcmena is newly in love, and married, and thus has eyes only for her husband, Jupiter decides to set up the following scam: he will come to her in the guise of her husband— indeed, a very strange approach for a lover, as commentators have already pointed out[2]—when Amphitryon, a Theban general, is fighting somewhere far away. In order to pull this off, Jupiter engages the help of Mercury, who takes on the appearance of Amphitryon's servant Sosie. Things get (comically) serious when Amphitryon returns early from his military expedition. In front of Amphitryon's house, Mercury holds the office of guard in Sosie's guise, while Jupiter (as Amphitryon) is entertaining Alcmena. The comedy starts when the "real" Sosie comes to the house, sent ahead by his master (the "real" Amphitryon) to announce their early return. A long comic dialogue (initiated by the exchange quoted above) develops between Sosie and Mercury—that is to say, between two Sosies. In Molière's version especially, Sosie's character is strongly defined and is the bearer of a particular, additional comedy, a "comedy of the ego," different in its mode from the comedy of errors that develops between Alcmena and her two husbands. The dialogue between the two Sosies is a real study of the ego; so let us take a closer look at this dialogue of egos.

MERCURY: Who goes there?

SOSIE: I.

MERCURY: Who, I?

SOSIE: I. [*To himself*] Courage, Sosie!

MERCURY: Tell me, what is your condition?

SOSIE: To be a man, and to speak.

MERCURY: Are you a master, or a servant?

SOSIE: As fancy takes me.

MERCURY: Where are you going?

SOSIE: Where I intend to go.

MERCURY: Ah! This annoys me.

SOSIE: I am ravished to hear it.

MERCURY: By hook or by crook, I must definitely know all about you,

you wretch; what you do, whence you come before the day breaks, where you are going, and who you may be.

SOSIE: I do good and ill by turns; I come from there; I go there; I belong to my master.

(*Amphitryon*, Act I, Scene II)

First the ego introduces itself, and does so by saying "I." To the question about its more specific identity, a correct Fichtean answer is provided: "I is I." And what is the fundamental condition of the ego?—To be a man, and to speak. It would be hard to put it better. Then comes the tricky question: is the ego a master or a servant?—both, in turn. Right again. As Lacan puts it in his brief commentary on the play, this is "a very pretty definition of the ego. The fundamental position of the ego confronted with its image is indeed this immediate reversibility of the position of master and servant" (Lacan 1988, p. 265). Let us move on: Where is the ego going?—Where it intends to go. Indeed, the ego goes where it intends to go, which is not to say (as the development of the play demonstrates) that it actually gets there. Then comes the exclamation, indicating the displeasure of one ego, followed by the affirmation of the other ego's pleasure—all this to indicate, it would seem, the close connection between the ego and the pleasure principle. And then again a series of more specific questions. What does the ego do?—Good and ill by turns. Again a reversibility that seems to be one of the ego's fundamental characteristics. And on it goes, along similar lines. . . .

After this study of the ego, Mercury decides to press harder to find out this other ego's name. And it turns out that the name is Sosie—in brief, that it is precisely the ego already occupied that night and in that place by Mercury. And since two egos cannot be in the same place at the same time, Mercury takes it upon himself literally to beat the other ego's out of his/its head. This is what follows (after the beating):

MERCURY: Well! Are you still Sosie? Why say you?

SOSIE: Your blows have not made any metamorphosis in me; all the change there is is that in the matter I am Sosie thrashed.

MERCURY: Still? A hundred fresh blows for this fresh impudence. . . .

MERCURY: Are you still Sosie? Say, villain!

SOSIE: Alas! I am what you wish; dispose of my lot exactly as you please: your arm has made you the master of it.

MERCURY: I think you said your name was Sosie?

SOSIE: True, until now I thought the matter was clear; but your rod has made me see that I was mistaken in this affair.

MERCURY: I am Sosie: all Thebes avows it. Amphitryon has never had other than me.

SOSIE: You, Sosie?

MERCURY: Yes, Sosie; and if anyone trifles with me, he must take care of himself.

SOSIE: Heavens! Must I thus renounce myself, and see my name stolen by an impostor? How lucky I am a poltroon! Or, by the death . . . !

(*Amphitryon*, Act I, Scene II)

It is obvious that Sosie is an ego that keeps secretly believing in its own identity even when the circumstances force him to deny it publicly. The real turn appears only when Mercury manages to confuse him "psychologically." He tells him, in the "first person," some more intimate things that only ego-Sosie knows, and the latter slowly starts to believe that this other, intruding ego is perhaps indeed "himself." Thus confused, he returns to the harbor, to his master, and tells him that he could not reach Alcmena. At this point the comedy of the ego attains some of its climaxes. When Amphitryon asks Sosie who stopped him from entering the house, Sosie replies:

SOSIE: Sosie; another I, jealous of your orders, whom you sent to Alcmena from the port, and who has as full knowledge of our secrets as I who am speaking to you.

And when Amphitryon expresses his doubts about what he hears, Sosie goes on:

SOSIE: No, Monsieur, it is the simple truth: this I was at your house sooner than I; and, I swear to you, I was there before I had arrived.

And a little further on:

AMPHITRYON: You have been thrashed?

SOSIE: Truly.

AMPHITRYON: And by whom?

SOSIE: Myself.

AMPHITRYON: You have thrashed yourself?

SOSIE: Yes, I; not the I who is here, but the I from the house, who whacks soundly.

(*Amphitryon*, Act II, Scene I)

Molière's anatomy of the ego here is in fact a showcase of a comic procedure and of its essentially double movement that gives rise to the properly comic object. The first movement is the deconstruction of the imaginary Unity (or Oneness), in this case that of the ego as an imaginary formation that "expresses" personality (its outer appearance as well as its experiences accumulated with time). Sosie's ego splits into two Sosies (who look the same and have the same history of experiences—Mercury manages to prove to Sosie that he knows things that he could not know, were he not indeed Sosie himself), and through this procedure it is closely but surely stripped both of its image and of its experience, with no unity or substantiality. This part of the procedure is indeed very likely to warm our postmodern blood: identity is always a construction, if not pure fantasy; the subject does not exist, but is only a name for an assemblage of heterogeneous symbolic and imaginary procedures or determinations; there is no One, there is only multiplicity. . . . Yet this is only the first part of the comic movement, which in itself does not yet constitute comedy—along with it there is also another movement. For what is actually happening in the play? What is happening is exactly what I described in Part I as the properly comic procedure of replacing the imaginary One—not with a multiple, but with a short circuit between two constitutively exclusive sides of reality, that is to say, with an impossible (and sustained) link between them. Also—and related to this—in the very moment when the I/ego is stripped of all its properties, when it remains only as an empty word, as a pure signifying marker of the speaker, we see how—far from becoming a pure free-floating monad within the multiplicity of others—the "I" is irreducibly fastened to the other (to the "I" of an other). Comedy does not consist simply in the imaginary One falling apart, splitting into multiplicity or into two, but begins only at the moment when we see how these two can precisely not separate or part completely, and become simply "two ones." There is something like an invisible thread that keeps linking them, and it is this very thread that constitutes the true comic object. Hence the comic nature of lines such as: *I swear to you, I was there before I had arrived*. This line is funny or comical precisely because the play makes it possible, since it is not simply meaningless, or an abyssal logical paradox, but the most accurate description of the facts.

Sosie's first waggish retort (*Who goes there?*—I [moi]) retrospectively turns out to be an ominous prediction of his subsequent (comic) fate. The comedy will show him what he actually said, and will slowly reduce him to nothing but this "I," demonstrating for him what it means "to be I," "to be an ego"—namely, to be just anybody.

There is yet another crucial comic feature at work in the long initial dialogue between Sosie and Mercury–Sosie. What constitutes the fundamental oddness, the bizarreness of this dialogue?— The fact that it is constructed entirely around the theme of the double (*semblable*), yet what is strikingly absent from this dialogue is precisely the theme of resemblance. Mercury is a god, and there is little doubt that he could take on Sosie's exact appearance, resembling him in every minute detail (just as Jupiter appropriated

Amphitryon's image and fooled his wife with it). Yet Sosie meets his double, a spitting image of himself, and engages with him in a long existential dialogue on "being and ego," "being and I-ness," allows himself to be beaten up by him, then listens to his arguments. . . . And only towards the end, once Mercury has already convinced him with his arguments (that is, with his surplus-knowledge), does Sosie make a rather cursory observation to the effect that this other Sosie looks curiously like himself. Dramaturgically speaking, this oddity could be explained by the fact that the scene takes place at night (as it does in Plautus's version). Yet even if, for different reasons, that scene *has to* take place at night, the comic writer could have easily, say, put a torch in Sosie's hand, or made use of some other possible source of light in front of the house. In short, the absence of an immediate imaginary register of recognition could not be an accident, but is very much part of the comic procedure supporting the dialogue at stake. This peculiarity can be recognized as a crucial element of (at least) two important and related comic procedures. First, it is a direct consequence of Sosie's ego being taken not as an imaginary unity of his personality but as his unary trait, as the one and only characteristic of Sosie. Sosie's ego is not the name of the sum of different layers and characteristics of Sosie's personality, but appears as *one of the features of his character*—more precisely, as its main feature, as the principal oddity of his character.

This flagrant nonimportance of the likeness between the two Sosies is also part of another comic procedure that consists in flagrantly ignoring not only resemblance, but everything that immediate sensory perception is telling us. Two other comic examples immediately spring to mind. The first is from the Marx Brothers' *Duck Soup*. Chico enters Margaret Dumont's room disguised as Groucho (in order to obtain the war plans she is keeping in her safe), at which point Harpo enters, also disguised as Groucho; Chico hides under her bed, allowing Harpo to go on with his act. When Harpo–Groucho leaves the room, Chico–Groucho reappears, and when Margaret Dumont tells him she has just seen him leave "with my own eyes," he replies: "*Well, who you gonna believe—me or your own eyes?*"

A very similar constellation takes place in Georges Courteline's play *Boubouroche* (1893; little known outside France):[3] a man catches his wife with her lover, yet his anger is soon overshadowed by her own, as she insists that what he has seen did not take place. Her outraged arguments could be summed up very well as follows: "Who are you going to believe, my words or your own eyes?"

In Sosie's case, however, the matter is slightly different or redoubled: Sosie ignores the sense-certainty of the image of the other, whereas the other (Mercury) tries to make him doubt the sense-certainty of himself, of his "I." And in this respect, Sosie takes the attitude of a philosopher:

SOSIE: I begin to doubt myself in earnest. He has already cowed me into believing him to be Sosie; and he might even reason me into thinking him so. Yet, when I touch myself, and recollect, it seems to me I am myself. Where can I find some light that will clearly make my way plain? What I have done alone, and what no one has seen, cannot be known to anyone else; that, at least, belongs to me.

(*Amphitryon*, Act I, Scene II)

Do not these lines sound strangely like something out of Descartes's *Meditations*? Indeed, if we leaf through this founding book of modern philosophy—which establishes an ontological certainty precisely through a reduction of the ego to a pure point of enunciation stripped of all (imaginary) qualities and sensations, a mere point that utters "I"—we can find more than a few similarities with Sosie's mediations. In view of this, one could perhaps say that by putting the imaginary register aside, Molière proposes precisely the comedy of the Cartesian subject: the comedy of the subject as the place of enunciation. What happens if "my" place of enunciation is outside myself? For Lacan, this is precisely what is at stake with the notion of the subject: the point of enunciation does not coincide with "myself" or with my "ego." And the moment this becomes obvious, a comic effect occurs. Sosie speaks and talks "outside himself"—that is to say, outside the "ego" which tries to establish, through touching itself, that it is really "I."

Returning to the question of the relationship between "eyes and words," between the immediate certitude of sensible perception and the symbolic register of words, one should stress the following. What is at stake is not simply that, in examples like those mentioned above, comedy ridicules this strange power of the word, which presents us with a reality different from what it in fact is. Or—to put it more precisely—if comedy "makes comedy" out of this point, this in no way implies that it is itself simply taking the side of sense-certainty, defending it from the supposedly absurd effects of the Symbolic. Not only is comedy itself highly dependent on this power of the word, it is also very well aware that there is ultimately more truth (I should perhaps say: more room for truth) in "exterior words" than there is in immediate or inner feelings. In fact, we should go even further: not only does comedy know that there is usually more truth in words than in immediate sensations and perceptions, it also knows that, in the end, this is precisely what is comical. It is not simply the discrepancy between sense-certainty and words that "obviously distort" it that is truly comical but, rather, the fact that, all things considered, we shall come closer to the truth if we keep following the words.

Let us take an example that seems to contradict this point: *Tartuffe*. Tartuffe is a fraud and a hypocrite who never stops pretending to be something other than he is; and it seems indeed that the whole comedy is constructed around this simple discrepancy. If we look at it more closely, however, we notice two important things. First, the central comic character of the play is not Tartuffe but Orgon, whose main characteristic is precisely his blind and infallible belief or faith in Tartuffe, in each and every word the latter utters (a belief in all his "pretense"). And as long as he believes him he is not only the central comic character, but also the only happy character. For at the end he gives in under the pressure of his family, who keep insisting that words are deceptive, and that he should trust only his own eyes: he has to see with his own eyes how Tartuffe is seducing his wife, and the moment he starts to believe his own eyes, he loses both his comic quality and his happiness (that is to say, he loses Tartuffe). This final willingness to open his eyes (and rely on them) might seem quite natural, and the only possible ending for this kind of comedy or comic character. Yet how very differently Orgon could have reacted! For instance, he might have responded to the obvious and ultimate evidence of Tartuffe's betrayal with something like the closing line from *Some Like It Hot,* quoted above: "Well, nobody's perfect!"

As for Tartuffe, at the point where he himself is comical we are dealing with a very similar additional turn of the screw. Bergson has made a brilliant observation to this effect apropos of the masterful scene in which Tartuffe appears for the first time (which, by the way, is not until the beginning of Act III). Tartuffe steps out of the house and notices Dorine. He pretends not to see her, and cries out to his valet (who is supposedly in the house): "Lawrence, put up my hair-cloth shirt and scourge!" The instruction is designed, of course, solely for Dorine to "overhear," and to draw the desired conclusion: Tartuffe is a really holy man who spends his time ascetically flagellating in solitude. There is no reasonably good performance of this play in which the quoted line would fail to provoke gales of laughter. Why? Is it simply because we see clearly enacted the discrepancy between truth and semblance, between sense-certitude and words? Bergson suggests a much more insightful and convincing explanation:

> [Tartuffe] knows Dorine is listening to him, but doubtless he would say the same if she were not there. He enters so thoroughly into the role of a hypocrite that he plays it almost sincerely. Were it not for this material sincerity, were it not for the language and attitudes that his long-standing experienced as a hypocrite has transformed into natural gestures, Tartuffe would be simply odious. . . . (Bergson 1999, pp. 130–131)

This is indeed a brilliant insight into the functioning of the comical. Were Tartuffe not himself materially caught up in his own willful and studied appearance and words, he would not be comical at all. The comic Tartuffe is not the true (or "real") person behind the deceptive appearances that he so diligently spreads all around himself, but the Tartuffe whose truth is ultimately caught in these very appearances, and hence lies precisely in these appearances: that is, the Tartuffe of the *material sincerity* of his lying and his deceptions themselves.

In other words, what is comical is not simply how words can move a very long way from sense-reality, how they can be completely detached from it, but, rather, the fact that, even in this detachment, they still function pretty well, and produce material effects of truth. What is comical is not simply their disjunction but, rather, the "impossible" points of their joint articulation.

In discussing Orgon above, I briefly touched upon the issue of happiness. This issue does indeed involve some crucial aspects of comedy. The question of happiness—or, taken more generally, of satisfaction (that is, of the relationship between demands or desires and their satisfaction)—in comedy is closely linked precisely to the question of blind trust. One of the essential characteristics of comic characters (or at least of a certain type of comic character—I pointed out a significant exception in the last chapter) is their unshakeable trust in what we might call their metonymic object, or in the other that carries this object. In his lessons on aesthetics, Hegel points out that to the comical belong an infinite good humor and trust. It is this unshakeable trust that establishes the ground, so to speak, for a possible (happy) encounter of demand and satisfaction, which are usually in the habit of missing each other. To put it differently, this trust or blind faith opens up a scene for that relationship between the two, which by definition "doesn't exist," since there is no formula or Law that would guarantee or make possible any steadiness or regularity of the relationship between them. The "solution" invented by comedy is precisely not an invention of a miraculous formula that would change this nonrelationship into a relationship; rather, it is one of crediting the other. This implies that we do not trust the Other because we take her to be trustworthy, or because reasons for trust exist in the Other. On the contrary, trust is precisely what comes at the point of the lack in the Other, of the Other's inconsistency and inconstancy. The subject thus credits the Other precisely at the point where the latter escapes reciprocity and predictability.

The comic subject believes in his or her metonymic object, and this belief always contains an element of naivety. In the course of comedy, this belief usually and frequently turns out to be unjustified (that is, without any ground in the object/Other), and hence "naive." Yet it would be completely wrong to say that it is this (revealed) naivety that makes a character comical—that we are laughing at his or her naivety. The paradox that constitutes the core of the comical is, rather, this: although the unshakeable faith in the Other turns out to be unjustified, or at least very much out of proportion, the comic subject is not simply a victim of his naivety; on the contrary, it is this naivety itself that ultimately makes it possible for him to come into his own—that is, to find some satisfaction. And this is precisely what strikes us as comical: not that somebody turns out to be a poor fool who naively believes in his metonymic object, although it is clear to everybody else that the latter is not in the least trustworthy, and that (for example) it is merely playing games with the comic character, leading him by the nose, but the fact that this naivety itself makes it possible for the subject nevertheless to find some—from the rational point of view—unexpected, "out-of-place" satisfaction.

We would completely misunderstand this comic device if we were to see in it simply a variation on the theme of the incompatibility of happiness and knowledge, a variation on the theme "the more we know, the less happy we are," a promotion of "blessed ignorance.". . . The pivotal point in this affair is not knowledge, just as trust is not simply ignorance. The pivotal point is, rather, something that could best be summed up in Lacan's homonymic slogan, which also constitutes the title of one of his seminars: *les non-dupes errent*,[4] non-dupes err—those who refuse to be duped at any price are the biggest dupes; those who will do anything not to be fooled (or "made fools of") are the biggest fools; those who try to make absolutely sure that they do not fall prey to any appearance, semblance, or illusion are taken in to begin with. Why, and what does this mean? In the relationship between the subject and the Other there is a gray zone that can never be completely eliminated. It could be described as the zone of incalculability (of the effects of our actions, or motives for the actions of the Other), or simply the point of the "lack of the Other"—that is to say, the point that is not consistently covered, in advance, with the causal net structuring intersubjective relationships; the point that belies all notions of a possible perfect symmetry and/or reciprocity of the subject and the Other (or notions of a possible complete determination of the one through the Other). The reason for this is, paradoxically, the fact that this is precisely the point at which the subject is pinned to the Other, where she is pinned to the lack in the Other by her own lack. Trusting, crediting, the Other refers to and concerns this very point. For the subject's trust is not simply something which comes to the place of her knowledge or ignorance, but concerns knowledge of the Other. Or, to formulate this in terms of the previous discussion: those who are obsessed with avoiding all deception, and naivety, are precisely those who ultimately blindly believe that the Other knows exactly what she is doing, that is, is perfectly consistent in her existence and actions. This kind of disbelief (or mistrust) is the other side of the belief in a full (not "barred"), consistent Other, the Other without a lack. Disbelief is belief in one's own autonomy as guaranteed by the consistency of the field of the Other. And this kind of incredulity is ultimately a way of keeping the signifier of our own lack as far away from us as possible, buried in the field of the Other. As for blind trust, on the other hand, it is precisely not a simple belief in the Other's consistency, but it brings something else to the fore: the noncoincidence of knowledge and truth.

Real trust, as opposed to knowledge (especially knowledge based on sense-certainty), is always redoubled, it is never simply immediate. If we trust somebody, say, to return the money we lent him, this trust does not consist in our knowing, or being certain in advance, that we'll get our money back. It is, rather, that trust always somehow precedes itself, there is something objective or object-like about it, it is not simply a psychological state. We could say that in trust, the object always precedes the subject: trust is first objectified in the very stake, in what I already give the Other, and this is then followed by the subjective side of trust, a "blind faith" in this same metonymic object. (Comic) trust is thus always a trust in trust, which is what creates a time and place for the dimension of truth to eventually arise in the interval existing in this redoubling.

And is this not precisely the comical aspect of transference in psychoanalysis? This peculiar emergence of a "subject supposed to know," this presupposition that the Other knows the truth about the subject's unconscious desire, this automatic love for the analyst, is certainly not without its comic dimension. Yet what is this presupposition based upon? Not on the fact that the analyst has the opportunity to impress us by giving proof of her omniscience, but precisely on a mysterious *object* that we "see" in her. Lacan introduced his conceptualization of transference with a reading of Plato's *Symposium*, in which he emphasizes the notion of *agalma*, the mysterious surplus-object, "something in himself more than himself," that Alcibiades ascribes to Socrates. He relates this to his concept of the object *a*. It is precisely this treasure, situated in the Other, that activates the transference of knowledge; it is, so to speak, an objectified trust, later to be followed by subjective trust. The presupposition of the analyst's knowledge is not exactly "objective" but, rather, "object-related," fixed to an object—it is "blind faith" in the object-cause of the subject's desire, which is situated in the Other. Yet in spite of—or perhaps precisely because of—its blindness, it functions in such a way that it produces, in analysis, real effects of knowledge and truth.

THE OTHER AND THE OTHER

The theme of the double is indeed one of the great comic themes. Yet there is an important difference between the situation with which we are dealing in the case of Sosie, and another which is actually much more common and frequent: the one in which doubles and twins do not come across each other (that is, across "themselves")—until the end, and this with the purpose of re-establishing the difference, of recognizing their true identities. Moreover, in this latter case it is the very condition of comedy that these doubles do not meet directly, and that they do not know about each other's existence. In *Amphitryon* we have both kinds of doubles: Amphitryon himself is in the standard position of never meeting his double (until the end), but constantly running into the effects his double has produced in his own world. And this is the generative point of comedy in this case. If Amphitryon knew there was another Amphitryon going around his house and mess-ing with his wife, Alcmena's enthusiastic words to him about how great a time they had the previous night (when he had not been there at all) would not be comical. One thus has to distinguish be-tween Sosie's type of the double and this other standard comic theme, presenting us with a redoubling or multiplying of identi-ties, and with their confusion. In this genre of mistaken identities, the encounters are always crosswise—the characters meet their doubles only at the end. This situation is very well described by Shakespeare himself at the end of *The Comedy of Errors*:

I see we still did meet each other's man;
And I was ta'en for him and he for me;
And thereupon these errors are arose.
(Act V, Scene I)

Sosie, on the other hand, meets himself in the very first scene; his comedy is not about mistaken identity, it is, rather, about the iden-tity (of the ego) *as such*. Sosie is not taken for somebody else, for another person (or "ego") who happens to bear a strong resem-blance to him; he is taken, literally, for himself. This other ego is his ego (it is not somebody else's), and instead of going around confusing other people (as Amphitryon's other ego does), it keeps confusing Sosie himself.

If in the case of Sosie it is the ego (or the identity as such, "in itself") that is subjected to comic treatment and exhibited as an object, then in the case of comedies of "mistaken identity" there is something else. What? The *correlation* between (symbolic) identity and its (physical) bearer. That is to say: what is subjected to the comic treatment is the Other as the guarantee of a fixed or steady correlation between "someone" and his or her symbolic identity. In this case, the comic suspense is a suspense/suspension of the Other. During the time of a comedy of errors—that is to say, of mistaken identities—the Other sort of pulls out, as if it were suspended somewhere below the ceiling. At the same time—and as in the mechanism of classic suspense—it is our surplus-knowledge (about who is really who) that keeps it suspended: that prevents the Other from simply disappearing below the horizon, and the action from turning into a series of completely nonsensical events (which would happen if we did not know how things really stand). The term suspense/suspension is to be taken in its original emphasis on a *temporary* "hanging in the air," that is to say—as the *Oxford English Dictionary* has it—"temporary deprivation of one's office or position." In comedy of mistaken identities the Other is, so to speak, temporarily deprived of its office or position, and it (usually) reemerges only at the end, in order to set right what has been out of joint during the comic play, and to say: You are this, and you are that, the whole thing was a misunderstanding, and now everything is all right and in its place again. End of comedy, and back to work! This brings us to a frequent criticism according to which this kind of comedy is basically conservative, that it turns the world order upside-down only in order ultimately to reestablish it in its full force, with no cracks to speak of. I will address this issue below; for the purposes of the present discussion it is important to emphasize that the possibility of the eventual return of the Other is the inherent condition of this kind of comic suspense, whose function we have by no means exhausted.

So, let us continue: the Other is thus not simply dismissed, "fired," it is suspended, it floats somewhat above the scene, without being able to exercise its influence on it; it remains just close enough for the whole thing not to fall apart into something utterly absurd, yet it is left without the capacity to intervene. In this respect the Other is, in effect, an impotent Other, and this can tell us something about one of the pivotal points of this kind of comedy. When we are laughing at what is happening on the stage, at the endless, stretched and "overstretched" misunderstandings ("Oh, shit! He doesn't know he is talking to her! Hahahaha . . ."), are we not also laughing at something else at the same time? On one level we are, of course, laughing at someone on the stage babbling something to the "wrong" person; or at this person who has no clue what the other is talking about, or knows only too well. . . . Yet is it not quite obvious that behind or beyond these characters (and somehow also together with them) we are also laughing at something else: at the Other, hanging, dangling suspended in the air, powerless to do anything, to stop or clear up this mess and confusion, unable to exercise its "office," its function? In this respect, a classic comedy of errors would always seem to involve a certain derision of the Other.

But perhaps derision is not the best word to describe the rather complex dimension of what is going on. For what is the difference between derision and a proper comic pleasure? Perhaps the simplest way of defining this difference would be the following. Derision is a constellation in which we are shown the Other as not being up to its task (in which we are shown the Other as "lacking," malfunctioning, and so on) in such a way that this lack or failure is funny in itself. The emphasis is thus on producing and displaying the funniness of the inconsistency/failure of the Other. Comedy proper, on the other hand, puts the emphasis somewhere else—it is a constellation in which it is not this failure of the Other in itself that is funny; rather, it is that funny things happen because the Other is not up to its task. In other words, the emphasis is on the surplus, material side of the situation—it is on the level of the latter that the comedy of accidents, surprising encounters and outcomes, hilarious dialogues, productive misunderstandings, and so on, is being played out.

In this perspective one could also say that the comic suspense of the Other functions in such a way that the suspension of the symbolic Other coincides with the surprising appearance of a (small) other: in the form of a double or in the form of a surplus comic object that could be defined (in comedies of error) as "error incorporated." This surplus comic object is not simply this or that object that we see in the play but, rather, something like an objective surplus of error which sticks to different protagonists at different moments, implicating them in all sorts of comic situations; or the protagonists keep handing it on to each other like a hot potato.

This can help us to further define the specific mode of comic suspense. For what is the difference between the suspense that we know, say, from classic thrillers (or "suspense movies") and comic suspense? As the word itself already indicates, suspense is a tension, an exciting and anguished expectation constituted and maintained by the fact that its crucial elements are not realized but remain "in the air" as a possibility and/or a threat. In relation to the real force of this imminent threat, the hero usually has an extremely narrow escape; he "only just" escapes. Comic suspense, on the other hand, springs not from such a suspended realization but, rather, from an overrealization or a prerealization. What makes and inaugurates a comedy is that something like a hot potato immediately falls from the cataclysmic sphere which, in classic thrillers, hangs above the protagonists like a menacing cloud. The comic suspense is all in the question of how the protagonists will deal with this "hot potato," how they will manage it, handle it, what they will do with it; where it will burn them; how far (and in what directions) they will go to avoid being burned; how it will catch up with them nevertheless. . . . A prototype of comic suspense is not the question if and when the husband will discover the proverbial lover in his wife's closet; rather, it is *what will hap-*

pen after he does. To be sure, comedy as a dramatic genre may well include the procedures of classic suspense, yet these are to be distinguished from comic suspense proper, which is in fact a paradoxical "suspense after the fact": it starts only at the moment when the catastrophe (or some portion of it) has already happened. The suspense of the Other coincides with the emergence of a surplus-object (as if the latter were in fact an irreducible objective kernel of the former), a not-quite-predictable action, the effects of which form the inner tension (suspense) of comedy.

This has an important further implication: the destiny of this object in the play, as well as the destiny of the play as propelled by this object, is not without consequences for the (suspended) Other, so that when it returns to its office, it might not be simply the same as before. While suspended, the Other is not simply absent from the scene: it is absent as the symbolic frame of Sense, yet very much present as a surplus-object of nonsense, so to speak. And comic nonsense sometimes has a startling way of making sense, that is, of "making other sense." Through different plots and situations, comedy is thus also a practice demonstrating that the Other (as the symbolic presupposition of sense) is no ideal or eternal and unchangeable in its form; via the surplus-object, it is always irreducibly attached to and involved in concrete reality, it is finally as dependent on the latter as the latter is dependent on it. If the Other "forgets" this, comedy is quick to drag it onto the stage in the form of a (small) other, in the form of a surplus-object—that is to say, in the form of that "hot potato" whose passing around will not be altogether without consequences for the symbolic functioning of the Other.

Good examples of this are two classical comedies of mistaken identity: Molière's *Amphitryon* (in that segment of the plot that concerns not so much Sosie but Amphitryon) and Shakespeare's *Comedy of Errors*. In both cases we can see how the authors "used" this comic configuration in order to think through and articulate a certain historical and social shift in the symbolic Other. It is characteristic of both plays that the final return of the Other (from its suspension) is far from reaffirming the Other (the symbolic co-ordinates) with which the plays begin.

First, *Amphitryon* is an excellent example of our thesis according to which the comic suspense of the Other does not simply mean that the Other is absent from the scene: it is absent as the symbolic frame of Sense (guaranteeing the symbolic identities), yet very much present as the surplus-object of nonsense. For in this comedy, the suspension of the Other (of Jupiter, "the boss of it all") from his heavenly office directly coincides with his appearance on the stage in the form of a surplus-other—of one husband too many, of an additional Amphitryon. And his presence on the stage of events in this object-like form has considerable effects on the overall symbolic structure when it is reestablished at the end, as well as on the subjects of this structure. The misunderstanding that misled Alcmena is of course cleared up; she had no means of distinguishing between her husband and Jupiter's clever imper-sonation of him, yet—and this "yet" is quite huge—Alcmena is pregnant! The suspension of the god, his vacation on the earth, was definitely not without real consequences—not only for Alc-mena, but for the status of the symbolic authority as well. Al-though the ending in Molière's version differs considerably from the ending of Plautus's *Amphitryon*, they nevertheless share one important feature: that of introducing a certain level of equality between two (previously) incommensurable symbolic ranks. In Plautus, this leveling appears between Jupiter and Amphitryon, between god and man. Alcmena is pregnant not with one child, but with twins, and gives birth to them before the play is over. One is from the god, the other from man. And, as Jupiter puts it in the end: "These two, my own and yours, she bore together" (Plautus 1995, p. 64 [1184]). Amphitryon has the last word in the play; he is triumphant, he bears no grudges—indeed, he is "hon-ored to have shared my goods with a god" (ibid., p. 62 [1171]). So, although Jupiter returns to his heavenly office, this affirma-tion of equality remains echoing on the stage in gloriously tri-umphant tones.

In relation to this, Molière's ending is quite different, and indeed unexpected. There is no reconciliation between Amphitryon and Jupiter, no symbolic settlement or appeasement. Amphitryon, the "master on earth," does not reassume his symbolic office, he does not have the last word; as a matter of fact, he has no word, no speech at all. A deafening "silence of Amphitryon" marks the last two scenes of the play—which are the scenes of clearing up the misunderstandings by revealing the true identity of Mercury and Jupiter. It is only Sosie, the servant, who speaks: not only when it is indeed his turn or place to speak and to settle the accounts with his double, Mercury, but also in the last scene with Jupiter, where he clearly takes the place in the dialogue that should have been occupied by his master, Amphitryon (who is present, but silent). What takes place in this last scene is a leveling not between god and man, but between master and servant. And it is by no means glorious but, rather, embarrassing, the servant taking it upon himself to save what is left of his master's humiliated face.

When Jupiter turns up again as Jupiter, he explains who he is, that he has taken Amphitryon's image in order to sleep with his wife, trying to impress upon Amphitryon (this time obviously with much less success) how great an honor this really is. . . . His speech is interrupted by Sosie's sarcastic remark ("The Seigneur Jupiter knows how to gild the pill"), after which Jupiter goes on with his self-important babbling, announcing that Alcmena is pregnant, that she will give birth to Hercules, who "shall cause the vast universe to ring with his deeds." To ease the embarrassment that this arrangement might cause in Amphitryon's household, he promises Amphitryon "a glorious future crowned with a thousand blessings." When he finishes his speech, Naucrates, a soldier, opens his mouth to acknowledge and affirm this glory, but Sosie cuts him short with the following curious, intriguing speech, which concludes the play:

SOSIE: Gentlemen, will you please take my advice? Do not embark in these sugary congratulations; it is a bad speculation; phrases are embarrassing on either side, in such a compliment. The great God Jupiter has done us much honor, and, unquestionably, his kindness towards us is unparalleled; he promises us the infallible happiness of a fortune crowned with a thousand blessings, and in our house shall be born a brave son. Nothing could be better than this. But, nevertheless, let us cut short our speeches, and each one retire quietly to his own house. In such affairs as these, it is always best not to say anything.

(*Amphitryon*, Act III, Scene X)

This is exactly what Amphitryon does: he keeps his mouth shut, as any clever *servant* would have done under the circumstances (we should not overlook the fact that what happens to Amphitryon has a clear resonance with an old story, only casting the roles slightly differently: the story of a master who has his way with a maid and who, after making her pregnant, goes to the trouble of explaining to her servant husband that he should in fact feel flattered, and that he will provide for his son's education and future . . .). Amphitryon doesn't say a word; the servant takes his place and speaks. To say what? Basically: *Gentlemen, cut the crap!* Stop this mawkishness; what happened is not very nice, but let's look at things from the practical angle. Jupiter promises us infallible happiness, fortune, a thousand blessings, and a brave son. Isn't this what everybody wants? *Tout cela va le mieux du monde*, he says in the original—this is all fine and great, it couldn't be better; the irony is more than just implicit. But enough of talking: go home and back to work, and not another word about this unpleasant matter.

This is indeed an intriguing specimen of a monologue that fuses the position of the master and that of the servant, as if to confirm the thesis of their reversibility. This is how we could understand Lacan's hint that the real doubles or "twins" in this play are not so much the two Sosies and the two Amphitryons but, rather, Sosie and Amphitryon, the master and the servant (Lacan 1988, p. 270). Is this fusion and/or reversibility not also marked in Sosie's final monologue by the fact that he ceases to appear as "I," the ego, and becomes "us" (Jupiter has done *us* much honor, his kindness towards *us* is unparalleled, he promises *us* infallible happiness, in *our* house shall be born a brave son, let *us* cut short our speeches)? The reversibility of the position of the master and of the servant seems to get stabilized in the figure of a "we/us," *nous*, as, in this case, literally the double figure, the figure of a master-servant. Brothers-in-injury, the master and the servant appear on the same level.

The Other that is reinstated, restored at the end of this comedy of mistaken identities is not the symbolic register of the old Master whose place has been usurped, during the play, by the bantering god. Rather, it coincides with a definitive suspension of the Master, who is left with no say at all.

Something structurally very similar takes place in Shakespeare's *Comedy of Errors*. If we look at its opening and its conclusion, we can hardly miss not only the general configuration of the suspension of the Other, but also the shift in the Other to which this comedy gives form. In the first scene, we do not only learn all that is necessary for the understanding of the confusing action that follows (the pre-story of the two pairs of twins, of how the storm had separated them, and how since then they have been wandering around the world), we learn it from the mouth of the Father, Aegeon, who has the shadow of death hanging over him—he is under threat of immediate execution. By way of explanation of this drastic threat with which the comedy begins, we are told the following, rather bizarre story: due to numerous trading conflicts between the Syracusans and the Ephesians, both towns have passed a decree to the effect that any Syracusan seen in Ephesus (and, of course, vice versa) is to be executed immediately and his goods confiscated—except, that is, if he pays a thousand marks' ransom. This situation is very odd indeed, and it has to strike us as an almost embarrassingly direct way of staging the decline of the symbolic authority of the Other, which is being replaced by a life-and-death struggle among "small others"—and, of course, by commerce.

We thus have a father of twins (both Antipholuses) and a stepfather of another pair of twins (both Dromios), who has appointed the latter servants (*sic*) to the former. He is a merchant from Syracuse who shows up in Ephesus, and is now under threat of execution there. He is also the bearer of the knowledge about the identity of all the twins—that is to say, the Other whose disappearance would most probably result in drawing everyone concerned into an irretrievable vortex of chaos. So he is not eliminated, but suspended: although he does not have a thousand marks, the Duke of Ephesus, having heard his story of the lost twins, takes pity on him and suspends his death sentence for one day, in which he is to try to get hold of the required sum. With these words—

Hopeless and helpless doth Aegeon wend,
But to procrastinate his lifeless end.

(Act I, Scene I)

—the father leaves the stage, and reappears only at the end. The suspension of the Other is thus underlined by the temporary suspension of the death sentence which is about to befall him very soon, and which further emphasizes how the Other is about to collapse. And then starts the comedy of the two pairs of twins who, without knowing it, are all in Ephesus, where they keep missing one another and confusing other people with their identical appearance. For our present purposes we will leave this comedy aside and jump to the end of the story, its dénouement. Although, as I have already said, Aegeon reappears at the end, the central figure of the dénouement is not him but Aemilia, an abbess at Ephesus, who of course turns out to be none other than Aegeon's long-lost wife and the mother of the twins. Yet it is interesting to see what exactly is the price of this "turbo-happy ending" of family happiness and wholeness rediscovered: for in order for the thing to function again, the symbolic roles had to undergo a rather drastic change. The father will be saved from imminent death—not at the price of a thousand marks (the Duke exempts him from this payment at the end) but, again, at the price of silence and withdrawal, that is, at the price of losing what is called "traditional paternal authority." At the end, everybody gets to make this or that triumphant or reconciliatory speech; only the father, Aegeon, does not. His place is taken by his wife, who is the agent of the symbolic (and practical) reconciliation, as well as the generous hostess who invites everybody—from the twin servants to the Duke of Ephesus—to a feast, a *gossip's feast*. This hint at equality (at affinity or kinship-in-spirit instead of kinship-in-blood) is further strengthened in the famous last verses of the comedy, which ends with the dialogue of the servant pair of twins. At first, they still worry about the question of hierarchy and of the privilege due to the firstborn child, but they soon realize that as twins they will have a hard time determining who is to have the privilege of the older son. And after dismissing the idea of leaving this to chance ("We'll draw cuts for the senior . . ."), the play concludes with a triumphant affirmation of fraternity:

We came into the world like brother and brother;
And now let's go hand in hand, not one before another.
(Act V, Scene I)

This ending—which, as Mladen Dolar has pointed out, "sounds like a sentence from the declaration of Human Rights or a decree of the French Revolution" (Dolar 2005a, p. 190)—is again a good reminder of the fact that the Other does not always return intact from its comic suspension. Or, rather, it is a good indicator of how the mechanism and the dialectics of comedy can be used to confront us with or lead us through certain shifts in the symbolic Other.

It is important to emphasize again, however, that this eventual effect that, so to speak, the phenomenal order of things can have on its own transcendental conditions or horizon is strictly related to the occurrence of a comic object as the material subsistence of the symbolic Other. In other words, if the other side of the comic suspension of the symbolic Other were not the material presence on the scene of this Other in the form of a surplus-object, then this (retroactive) effect of the determined world on the very coordinates of this determination could not take place. And if we relate the notion of the comic object (as material surplus of a given situation) to the Lacanian concept of the object *a*, there are several interesting consequences for the status of the latter, especially in the perspective of the relationship between object *a* and the Other. If, by the Other, we mean the symbolic coordinates that structure our world, as well as providing its vocabulary, then what exactly is the object *a*? Like many other things that constitute our world, it is an effect of the Other, yet it is a very singular point of this efficiency. It is the point at which the effect maintains an "open line," in effect, with the symbolic structure that generates it, so that the latter remains dependent, "vulnerable," in relation to it. If symbolic causality is distinguished by a clear cut that implies an irreducible gap between cause and effect, then object *a* is a point where a cause immediately is (its own) effect. It is a paradoxical effect-cause—not in the sense of an effect which is in turn a cause of some further effect, but in the sense of their coincidence. In relation to desire, Lacan speaks of the object-cause of desire—but could one not also say effect-cause of desire? It is an object that is strictly speaking an effect of the structure of desire, it does not exist outside or prior to it, yet at the same time it is the bearer of the very causality of desire, the point where the structure is, so to speak, *alive*, and where its destiny is being played out "in real time." In psychoanalysis, this also resonates with the concept of the symptom: the symptom is an effect of a certain symbolically structured impasse, yet an effect in which the very causality that brought it about is kept alive. The symptom is, at the same time, a rather rigid form (or "ritual"), automatically triggered by certain circumstances, yet in all its rigidity and automatism it is also—to use the popular term—a constant work-in-progress, it is where the conflict is being constantly played out and repeated (in a form which provides the subject with some "impossible" satisfaction, enjoyment).

To return to our argument: the object *a* is a material sensitive point of a system, a point that comedy plays with abundantly. However, it is not enough to say, for example, that comedy treats this object in a comic or humorous way, whereas other genres may treat it in their own specific way. For the first distinguishing feature of comedy is that it produces it *as object* in the first place, or uses material which already has this "comic" quality. Things can have a comic quality without belonging to a comedy, and without being funny in themselves. Some very sad things can have a comic quality to them—which is precisely a quality related to an objectification of a feature that seems otherwise organically integrated to a given personality or situation.

If we formulated this in terms of *das Ding*, the pivotal yet inaccessible point of a given symbolic universe, we could say that in comedy, the Thing does not remain simply transcendent (and discernible only in its effects on subject). It is produced on the stage in an objectified, material form, as object-symptom of a given situation. This maneuver is often seen as a transformation of a real and irredeemable difficulty into a mere inconsequential banality, as an escape from whatever Real the Thing involves. This judgment, however, is very unjust to comedy, since it confuses comedy with something quite different, namely with derision, which is actually fully preoccupied with keeping the Thing untouched and unseen, by keeping it safely beyond. Not everything that provokes laughter is comedy, and there are certainly cases in which the object shown on the stage and proposed as an object of laughter is not a comic object at all in our sense of the word (a surplus of a given subject or situation which is the very embodiment of its fundamental antagonism), but functions instead as a smokescreen that prevents both the true object from emerging and the comedy from developing at all. What I have in mind is something that appears and thinks of itself as a gesture of subversive profanation, but is in fact the very opposite. The basic gesture it consists of is one of—"showing it." But showing what, exactly? A tongue, a butt, or a penis—these are the most common readymades used in this technique. As we are touching here upon things that demand to be treated with the utmost precision, the following specification is called for before we continue. This distinction between derision techniques and comic techniques lies not in the type of objects they choose to expose (the three mentioned above can very well have their place in comedy) but in the modality of this exposure. In derision techniques, the objects listed above are used in a manner that aims to stop the discussion and its inherent comedy, and to preserve the dignity of the Thing. What a gesture of this sort says is precisely: "Stop that comedy!" To take an example, let us imagine a group of philosophers passionately discussing an issue that may seem completely trivial to the so-called common man, like: "What is the nature of being?" While they are thus debating, a jester might be tempted to intervene in this "charade" with a gesture of derision—for example, by showing his butt. What is at stake in this gesture is not at all what one might call "making comedy"; instead, the gesture is one of *exposing* the "comedy" of the existing situation, with the aim of condemning it as such and putting an end to it. What is intolerable to the jester is precisely the implicit "comedy" of the situation, with its "embarrassing" pretension to seriousness. This is why I am tempted to say that this specific figure of the jester does not belong at all to the tradition of comedy and its way of engaging in "monkey business." Contrary to its "obscene" appearances it belongs, rather, to the ascetic tradition. This is most obvious in cases that might be described as cases of "compulsive derision": compulsive jesters tend to identify with the "real" (hidden, obscene) truth of a situation, they like to put themselves (or a part of their body) forward as the embodiment of this obscene underside as the locus of truth. The problem here, however, is that this all too willing display of what is usually ("culturally") meant to remain covered (a tongue, a butt, a penis . . .) functions, in most cases, as the *veil* of a perhaps more disturbing fact: that the comedy might not stop when we get to the "Real" behind it, but could continue there. In other words, "showing it" might be a way of protecting and veiling something else: the sacred mystery of a given symbolic structure, put in jeopardy by this or that "comic charade."

Before leaving this register of comedy, defined as "the other and the Other" and related to the figures of doubles, twins, or, more generally, to all kinds of identity confusion, we cannot avoid mentioning a specific master of this register: Marivaux. Marivaux is interesting for at least two reasons. First, because he adds to the discussed dialectics of "others and the Other" his own specific turn of the screw. And second, because he shifts the emphasis from doubles and twins to masking and cross-dressing as the primary source of identity confusion (which is the path taken by a substantial body of modern comedy). Marivaux is the great author of masquerade—not masquerade as opposed to truth, but masquerade as the royal way to truth. One could almost formulate Marivaux's motto as follows: "Everything is deceptive, only the mask never lies." The preoccupation with the dialectics of appearance and truth is so much in the foreground of Marivaux's universe that it completely overshadows individual characters. Indeed, it is hard to imagine a stronger contrast, in this respect, between Molière and Marivaux. On the one side we have powerful, fascinating, brilliantly constructed Characters, who almost carry the entire comedy in themselves. On the other side we have something that is almost like a pure structure (and dynamics of this structure), producing comedy with a mathematical precision and necessity, so that the individual bearers of this structure are practically irrelevant. One could define Marivaux as a "dialectical structuralist" among classic comedy writers; he is a proper mathematician of comedy who invented one fundamental axiom that he keeps repeating and testing from one comedy to another. There are many who criticize Marivaux for this repetition of the same axiom again and again, as well as for his insistence on pure structure. Yet although it is true that—once we have learned the trick—a consecutive reading of several of Marivaux's plays can become slightly tedious, the fact remains that there is a "trick"—he did invent something, and this something is worthy of attention. So, what does it consist in? To put it simply, it consists in correlating the suspension of the Other not with a surplus-object but with a pure difference, difference as inherent to identity.

Let us take the example of *Le jeu de l'amour et du hazard* (1730), probably the most quintessential of Marivaux's plays, and certainly the most successful. Here is the basic plot: With the numerous experiences of certain friends of hers in mind, Silvia determines not to accept Dorante, the suitor chosen for her, until she has had the opportunity to study him in secret. She therefore modifies her dress to suit the role of her maid Lisette, while Lisette assumes the role of the lady; but Dorante, who is not more willing to be mismatched than is Silvia, determines upon the same stratagem, and arrives in the livery of his servant Harlequin, who in turn is to play the part of the master. In this way we get a quadrangular structure, the terms of which are shifted out of line in relation to each other (a mistress, who is actually the maid; a maid, who is actually the mistress; a master, who is in fact the servant; and a servant, who is in fact the master). Both couples are, of course, ignorant of the fact that the other couple has also switched roles—apart from us, the spectators, only Silvia's father Orgon and her brother Mario have this surplus-knowledge, and thus the full picture. And this rather minimal, very simple structural configuration is enough to start and feed the engine of this pretty delirious comedy.

We could perhaps be tempted to raise the objection that this configuration is precisely *too simple* and not interesting enough, since it rests on a rather sentimental opposition between the Real and the Symbolic, between real love and the conventions prescribing in advance who is suitable for whom, marriage being cast as an institution entirely devoid of all genuine emotions. There is no doubt that this play is, among other things, an enlightened critique of arranged marriages, as well as of the confinement of (legitimate) love to the boundaries of the same social class (when

Dorante falls in love with Silvia, he is ready to marry her even though he believes her to be a maid, and he develops a whole argument in support; he is, however, somewhat relieved when she turns out to be the mistress). At the beginning of the play Silvia passionately explains to her maid why she has no taste for marriage: usually, there is everything in it but love; men show one face at home and another in society; outside their home they are all manners, charm, and wit, whereas at home they are cold, disagreeable, boring, if not simply nonexistent. Outside, and particularly when they are involved in seduction, they wear the most amiable masks; whereas at home with their wives they let their masks fall, and once a woman thus gets to know what her husband is really like, it is already too late. Hence Silvia's plan: she wants to get to know Dorante as he really is, and to observe how he will behave towards her as she really is, outside her role of the rich mistress whom he has to marry. As for Dorante, he is driven by the same motives: he wants to find out whether true love is possible between them. We could thus say that they both want to establish if the other could love them "such as they are," outside the symbolic roles and places where they already exist as a match. But how does a woman find out if the other loves her for herself alone? Here is the answer of Marivaudian comedy: by pretending to be somebody else. How do I find out if he really loves *me*? By dressing up as somebody else. If he falls in love with this somebody else, he loves me! The path to truth leads through fiction. Or, more precisely: we do not get to the Real by eliminating the symbolic fiction, the mask, and looking behind it, but by redoubling the symbolic fiction, the mask, by putting another one on top of the already existing one. The way to authenticity leads through double artifice and skill, the way to immediacy through double mediation, the way to the interior through a redoubled exterior. This is one of the fundamental "dialectical" truths of Marivaudian comedy. In spite of some resemblances, the Marivaudian universe of love is not the romantic universe: the latter actually reduces the configuration exclusively to the couple of the Real (genuine love) and the symbolic fiction/convention, and situates all truth of love on the side of the "Real." Marivaux, on the other hand, does something different: he situates the Real in the space of the pure inner difference produced by the redoubling of the fiction/convention.[5]

Marivaux is also a great master of this dialectics of redoubling in the relationship between the Imaginary and the Symbolic: what leads to the Symbolic is the redoubling of a first imaginary turn. Silvia and her maid switch places to become each other's mirror-images. If this were all—that is to say, if Dorante did not also switch places with his servant—we would be dealing with the classic configuration of the subject put to the test in which he has to be able to tell the true Silvia from the apparent one. Yet the first mirror-turn is redoubled by the second, in which Dorante changes place with his servant. In this way the protagonists actually find themselves (back) in their starting positions (Dorante with Silvia and Lisette with Harlequin), yet with an inherent, minimal, invisible difference constitutive of the Symbolic. The one who is testing the other is himself put to the test. And if they are to meet (happily), this can happen only within the space of this interval, where the ignorance of the one coincides with the ignorance of the other. Thanks to the redoubling, we leave behind the imaginary mirror-turn logic for another logic, that of an internal *shift*: we get a reality that is slightly out of place in relation to itself, a reality that is simultaneously ahead of itself and behind itself, a reality that is at the same time anticipating and lagging behind itself. This shift opens up the space for the symbolic Other as immanent to the given situation (as opposed to the Other constituting its framework or outer horizon).

This can help us to specify another mode of comic suspense, which differs slightly from the one I have already discussed: the suspension of the Other coincides with the emergence of a surplus-object, and the unpredictable ways of the latter constitute the comedy's inner suspense, as well as affecting the status of the (temporarily) suspended Other. In Marivaux, we are dealing with a different configuration. The suspended Other appears on the stage in the form of the inner difference of every identity, and the comic suspense turns around the question of how this or that identity will sustain this difference. We are not so much in the dynamics of sending back and forth a surplus ball as we are in the dynamics of testing the symbolic Other at the points of these inherent differences and intervals. In other words, the Other is tested as to what sort of rearrangements of the "small others" it still endures. Let us formulate this more concretely. Mixed and confused identities in Marivaux are mostly not—despite the preeminent role of the masquerade—in the service of a carnivalesque enabling of transgressions and the exploitation of their comic effects (in the sense of temporarily making the impossible possible: the servant beating and insulting the master, the mistress falling for the servant, and so on). As a matter of fact, Marivaux makes surprisingly little use of the potential of this immediate comedy of mixed identities. Instead, he abundantly plays the chords of the register of another question. Let us formulate it like this: is it possible, and to what extent, that the words of A, addressed to B, who is in fact C, are intercepted by the symbolic Other (in the form of the interval between B and C) in such a way that A and C will nevertheless reach an understanding? Or, more simply: how can the words addressed to a wrong other nevertheless be kept by the Other in the field of gravity of this same other as the right one?

From Leibniz we know the concept of "preestablished harmony," referring to the (God-provided) harmonized development of parallel monads that directs them to the same goal. Could we not say, in relation to this, that the axiom of Marivaux's universe is something like a *preestablished disharmony*: a discordance between monads on account of which things attain their true goal only by following the wrong path?

PART III

CONCEPTUALIZATIONS

ANOTHER TURN OF THE BERGSONIAN SCREW

Henri Bergson was one of those rare philosophers who dealt with the phenomenon of comedy at length, and dared to propose no less than its ultimate formula: *du mécanique plaqué sur du vivant*— something mechanical encrusted upon the living (Bergson 1999, p. 39). This is the formula that condenses and names, in one line, the two levels that Bergson isolates as fundamental compounds of the comical: on the one hand automatism, rigidity, inertia, uniformity, repetition; on the other vitality, live energy, elasticity, changeability (a smooth passage of one state into another). The latter is of course related to what Bergson, on the more general level of his philosophy, simply calls "life" or "life impulse" (*élan vital*) as the pure intensity of everlasting movement. The comic thus always implies a halt in the smooth run of life, of vividness; it is rigidity and automatism getting the upper hand over elasticity and impulse; it is—to use a terminology that is otherwise not Bergsonian—a state or Being that petrifies Becoming (as eternal movement). Whenever this happens before our very eyes, in a clearly visible, obvious way, the effect is comical.

Of course there have been writers before (and after) Bergson who emphasized the fact that the comical always seems to involve a certain encounter of two different (often directly opposed) levels or experiences. There is no lack of descriptive and occasional designations of these two levels, from rather abstract to very concrete ones. High–low, soul–body, mind–matter, artificial–natural, spirit–letter, human–animal, divine–human, ideals–reality, spontaneity–habit, culture–vulgarity, high aims–low needs . . . to name at random a few of these couples that appear frequently. The descriptions of the relationship in which comedy puts these two elements are also rather similar: one element (usually the "lower" one, but definitely the one that is veiled or even suppressed in a given situation) gets its breakthrough to the detriment of the other element, previously dominating or "usurping" the whole picture. Or, to put it in even more general terms: two elements which, because of their opposing tendencies and connotations, exclude each other (that is, exist in the mode of either/or, or as the other side of each other), are being posited on the same level, within the same horizon.

Bergson's gesture was not one of adding to the series above yet another couple, living–mechanical (or life–automatism); it was rather more ambitious. He (convincingly) proposed this couple as the real core or the "matheme" of all the others. A large part of his *Laughter: An Essay on the Meaning of the Comic* is dedicated to the attempt to demonstrate the reducibility of different descriptions of the comical to this conceptual matrix. To get a taste of it, let us look at two examples of Bergson's argument.

> In the first place, this view of the mechanical and the living dovetailed into each other makes us incline towards the vaguer image of *some rigidity or other* applied to the mobility of life, in an awkward attempt to follow its lines and counterfeit its suppleness. Here we perceive how easy it is for a garment to become ridiculous. It might almost be said that every fashion is laughable in some respect. Only, when we are dealing with the fashion of the day, we are so accustomed to it that the garment seems, in our mind, to form one with the individual wearing it. (Bergson 1999, p. 39).

> Let us suppose, however, that our attention is drawn to this material side of the body; that, so far from sharing in the lightness and subtlety of the principle with which it is animated, the body is no more in our eyes than a heavy and cumbersome vesture, a kind of irksome ballast which holds down to earth a soul eager to rise aloft. Then the body will become to the soul what, as we have just seen, the garment was to the body itself—inert matter dumped down upon living energy. The impression of the comic will be produced as soon as we have a clear apprehension of this putting the one on the other. And we shall experience it most strongly when we are shown the soul tantalized by the needs of the body. . . . (Bergson 1999, pp. 49–50)

I have chosen these two passages since, taken together, they show very nicely in what sense the Bergsonian formula of the comic is more formally conceptual than others, which often remain too empirical or content-determined. It implies a principle of flexibility that is often overlooked: it takes into account the fact that in the comic the same element can stand at the two sides of an opposition. Thus, in relation to clothes, "body" can occupy the position of liveliness and "spirit," whereas in relation to the spirit or "soul" it can occupy the position of an inert, dead thing.[1] This point, although Bergson does not make it completely explicit, can in fact be generalized: education and culture can function as liveliness of spirit as opposed to the inert materialism of natural needs, yet they can also function as a mechanical uniformity of social codes and constraints as opposed to the lively dialectics of physical needs. Moreover—and if one pushed the implications of the quotes a little further—one could say that all elements from the "higher" of the two oppositional series (spirit, mind, ideals, and so on) can appear as elements of the "lower" series, insofar as they appear as the rigidity that tries to frame the dynamic liveliness of the body, of needs, of reality, and so on. In fact, comedy is a constant reversing of the two series: now we laugh at a (physical) slip that undermines dignity, now we laugh at a dignity that strives to control such slips at all costs. We could even say that what is comical is this reversibility as such.

Bergson deserves full credit for this attempt to conceptualize the very difference that holds up both elements of comic opposition; this he does in terms of the difference between a configuration where "everything flows" (suppleness, absence of repetition, smooth and continuing change, elasticity), and another where "everything stands still" (rigidity, uniformity, repetition, automatism). The weakness of his theory, however, is that he stops his analysis at this point, cutting it short by relating the first modality to a very specific concept of "life" which comes from the wider background of his own philosophical edifice (*élan original, vital*), and relating the other modality to something that, historically speaking, fully escalated precisely in Bergson's time, penetrating all segments of human life: mechanics, and an overwhelming advance in establishing firm laws on all possible levels of existence. Perhaps it was none other than Freud who represented the peak of this movement, which encompassed, after establishing laws of the movement of matter and "things," also laws of life (the theory of

The Revolution of the Gatekeepers

evolution), of society (socioeconomic theories), of the human mind, and finally even of the unconscious. "Something mechanical (or lawful) encrusted upon the living" seems to be a formula that captures a most striking feature of the nineteenth century (especially of the last part). And it is hardly a coincidence that, as a kind of other side of the Bergsonian essay, which recognizes in this the generator of the comic, there is also a considerable, mostly literary corpus of the uncanny. Paradoxically, the latter also seems to fit the Bergsonian definition perfectly: something mechanical encrusted upon the living, the mechanical and the living dovetailed into each other. For what else is the stuff that the genre of the uncanny is made of—machines, automata that come to life, mortifying doubles, living dead . . . ?

The problem of Bergson's matrix is in no way that it is too narrow or reductive, but rather that it is too broad, not specific enough. Bergson is too quick to simplify the very complexity that he himself introduces. He simplifies it by decomposing it in an already existing dualism, in two preexisting layers which happen to meet only in the comical, while he completely overlooks the possibility of this duality already being a (retroactive) effect of the comical, not simply its elementary starting point. One should be even more precise: the comic movement does in fact reveal something twofold, a fundamental divergence in what is otherwise perceived as a harmonious or organic whole, and in this sense it could be said to point to an original, preexisting duality. Yet the problem is how to conceive of this duality. To conceive of it in terms of two completely independent and heterogeneous principles whose composition defines living beings is by no means the only option, nor does it spring from analysis of the comic as such.

The limit of Bergsonian analysis is in fact this aprioristic and rather abstract duality of his basic philosophical position, which perpetuates in more than one aspect the dualism of matter and spirit, body and soul, and in which body (inertia, automatism) inevitably falls on the side of what is imperfect and deficient. This is also why Bergson can ultimately define the phenomenon of laughter as nothing but, or more than, a mechanism of social corrective (of this imperfection).

> The comic is that side of a person which reveals his likeness to a thing, that aspect of human events which, through its peculiar inelasticity, conveys the impression of pure mechanism, of automatism, of movement without life. Consequently it expresses an individual or collective imperfection which calls for immediate corrective. This corrective is laughter, a social gesture that singles out and represses a special kind of absentmindedness in men and in events. (Bergson 1999, p. 82)

Challenging the supposition that sustains this view, we should ask whether inelasticity and inertia can really be treated as something *a priori* exterior to life, something that can only get "stuck," "tacked" or "encrusted" onto it. Is not the comic precisely the reversal in which we come upon something rigid at the very core of life, and upon something vivid at the very core of inelasticity? This is not to say that the figure of "tacking" or "encrusting" is itself problematic—on the contrary, it does convey a very important aspect of the comic. At this stage I would like to propose something else. What if the mechanical element in the comic is not simply one of its two poles or compounds, which is being "stuck," encrusted, on the other pole (on "life"), but could be said to refer to the very *relationship* between (any) two poles appearing as a "mechanical" relationship? A garment—to use the previous example—can strike us as being stuck, imposed on the body— not because it is so mechanical in itself, but because instead of the two fusing together into one graciously moving form, their relationship is perceived as purely exterior, "nonorganic," and in this sense "mechanical." In other words, it is the aspect of something (which might itself be perfectly vivid—or not) being stuck, tacked, encrusted onto something else that (already) embodies the mechanical side of the situation.

In order to illustrate and further elaborate on this suggestion, let us take an example analyzed by Bergson himself, which will help us make the difference between the two perspectives more evident. The example deals with the comic nature of imitation. It is indeed intriguing how a person's gestures, the way she speaks and moves, which do not seem particularly funny in themselves, can become extremely funny when somebody imitates them. And the better the imitation—the more the gestures are identical to those of their owner—the funnier they are. They are funniest when they are virtually indistinguishable from the "original," yet the "original" isn't funny, while its identical imitation is very funny indeed. (This, of course, can retroactively affect the original itself; once we have seen the imitation, the original, when seen again with its habitual gestures, can strike us as irresistibly funny.) Bergson explains this with the following argument. Our mental state is ever-changing, and if our gestures faithfully followed these inner movements, if they were as fully alive as we are, they would never repeat themselves. And they could not be imitated. He goes on:

> We begin, then, to become imitable only when we cease to be ourselves. I mean our gestures can only be imitated in their mechanical uniformity, and therefore exactly in what is alien to our living personality. To imitate anyone is to bring out the element of automatism he has allowed to creep into his person. (Bergson 1999, p. 34)

Bergson thus starts from a presupposition according to which our mental life is a pure movement and animation, divested of all inertia, automatism, and repetition, which consequently makes it very difficult for our material side (with its "obvious" inertia) to keep up with it, forcing it to resort to automatism. Automatism is a foreign body in our "living personality," the point where we cease to be ourselves. As ourselves (our living personality) we are not imitable or repeatable; what is imitable is only this mechanical foreign element (that has "crept" into our person).

This explanation is very much in tune with the exclusively "corrective" understanding of laughter, circumscribing it to the domain of derision, mockery, and scorn. This reduction, however, is highly questionable. Also, if we stop to think about some examples of comic imitation, is it not only too obvious how it brings out the fact that it is precisely in this "exterior" automatism that we are most "ourselves" (and not that we cease to be ourselves)? A good imitator always imitates precisely our singularity, the uniqueness of our tics and gestures, and of their combination. He imitates our very difference, specificity, individuality; he imitates our *inimitability*, and makes it a matter of repetition—it is precisely this that accounts for the comic effect.

We could indeed ask whether Bergson's pure "living personality" is not, rather, a fantasmatic screen at work in our everyday interactions with other people similar to us. Indeed, this element of similarity or likeness is in fact of crucial importance in our everyday *failure* to perceive the split or duality rendered perceivable through comic imitation. If the speech and the gestures of, say, the president of our country (that is, of our "parish") do not strike us as comic in themselves, but become so only when imitated, the speech and gestures of representatives of some other cultural parish, "foreign" to us, can strike us as immediately or "intrinsically" comic, without even being imitated. While watching them, we get the impression that these gestures are already imitating themselves; they strike us as inherently theatrical and they function as if they were already reflexively redoubled or coming from the outside. We immediately perceive in these "foreigners" what we fail to perceive in ourselves and in our fellow creatures, and what comic imitation reminds us of: the inherent rigidity of our own "living personality."

To return to our central argument: one could also, and perhaps more precisely, formulate what is at stake in the following way. According to Bergson, when we imitate someone, we necessarily leave out his or her "living personality," and imitate only what is already mechanical/imitable. Comic imitation would thus be a kind of (potentially infinite) extraction of the mechanical from the pure life with which it is entangled. Contrary to this, does it not ring more true to say that comic imitation reproduces all there is, yet by doing so—that is, by relating a habit to itself, by introducing something like a relationship in which this habit (when imitated) refers to itself—it produces pure life at its most obvious, as an object to be seen, as a thing?

Comic imitation is thus a very good example of the suggestion made above: the mechanical element in the comic is not simply one of its two sides or compounds, but the very relationship between the two (in this case the relationship of reproduction/ duplication, involved in imitation). What appears to be mechanical (habit) on the one side, and a pure fluid life on the other, are effects produced in this movement in which a life is referred back to itself, confronted (by means of imitation) with itself as seen from the outside. The crucial question is thus not: Is life reducible to mechanism? The question is: Is life reducible to itself? According to Bergson, it is. There is such a thing as a pure "immaterial" life. Yet the (conceptual) price of this assertion is that in its unblemished self-identity life becomes an ever-evasive, ungraspable leftover of everything that could actually be said to be. Life is what remains after we single out (for example, through imitation) everything there is. In other words: life is what is not. It exists only as an irreducible leftover of what is.

My stance is different: life is not (fully) reducible to itself, which is why it does not constitute transcendence to all there is but, rather, a crack in all there is. It is this noncoincidence of life with itself that takes the form of a relationship, and it is this relationship that can occasionally strike us as mechanical. It is in this sense that the mechanical is intrinsic to life, and cannot be satisfyingly conceptualized in terms of exteriority as opposed and foreign to a vivid spontaneous interiority. As a matter of fact, comedy has always exploited the register of the following question: To what extent is mechanical exteriority itself constitutive of the very liveliness of the "inner" spirit? Bergson's matrix runs in only one direction, which leaves out precisely this question. This is particularly striking in his discussion of the "comic element in words," which is based on the following presupposition: language is a means used by our inner thoughts and feelings to express themselves. And since it is imperfect, deficient as a means, since it does not have an organic life, but is full of mechanical operations, language can strike us as encrusted upon our spirit, betraying its signifying intentionality, unable to keep up with it. In short: living spirituality or living thought precedes all language, yet because it needs language to express itself, its passing from the inside out (through language) can produce all sorts of comic effects.

This conception completely ignores how much the "spirit" can be alive and at work precisely in puns, slips of the tongue, and plays on words. Just think of jokes: the wit in jokes could be defined precisely as "spirit produced by mere words." It concerns the productive dimension of language, not simply words failing to express a certain thought correctly.[2] It concerns the possibility of language itself (with its very mistakes and deficiencies) being productive of thought. When something like this happens, we don't laugh simply to mark and "correct" a linguistic fault or deficiency, we laugh at the "miraculous" occurrence of the surplus-sense that was produced from that very failure or nonsense. We don't laugh because spirit or thought failed to be expressed, or didn't get through correctly, we laugh because a thought or spirit did emerge, materialize "out of nothing" (but words). In other words, Bergson completely misses the dimension pointed out, for example, by Heinrich von Kleist in his brilliant essay "On the Gradual Production of Thoughts whilst Speaking." In this essay, Kleist points out a dimension best encapsulated by his own paraphrase of the French saying L'appétit vient en mangeant (appetite comes as one eats): L'idée vient en parlant (an idea emerges as one speaks). He thus draws our attention to the fact that when we begin a sentence, we often don't know exactly how it will end. In this case it is speech itself, with all its automatism (and with all the time-buying mannerisms and exclamations that are so perfect for comic imitation), that pulls the spirit along—the spirit slowly staggers behind the words, until it suddenly comes to life in an idea that has literally emerged with and from speech. Let us quote here one of Kleist's own great examples, garnished with his commentaries, which wonderfully bring out all the comedy of the given situation:

I believe many a great speaker to have been ignorant when he opened his mouth of what he was going to say. But the conviction that he would be able to draw all the ideas he needed from the circumstances themselves and from the mental excitement they generated made him bold enough to trust to luck and make a start. I think of the "thunderbolt" with which Mirabeau dismissed the Master of Ceremonies who, after the meeting of the 23 June [1789—the context is that of the beginning of the French Revolution], the last under the *ancien régime*, when the King had ordered the estates to disperse, returned to the hall in which they were still assembled and asked them had they heard the King's command. "Yes," Mirabeau replied, "we have heard the King's command."—I am certain that beginning thus humanely he had not yet though of the bayonets with which he would finish. "Yes, my dear sir," he repeated, "we have heard it."—As we see, he is not yet exactly sure what he intends. "But by what right . . ." he continues, and suddenly a source of colossal ideas is opened up to him, "do you give us orders here? We are the representatives of the nation."—That was what he needed!—"The nation does not take orders. It gives them."—"And to make myself perfectly plain to you . . ."—And only now does he find words to express how fully his soul has armed itself and stands ready to resist—"tell your king we shall not move from here unless forced to by bayonets."—Whereupon, well content with himself, he sat down.[3]

In relation to this example, we can of course also talk about the comic combination of "living spirit" and "automatism of language," yet what is comical is precisely their mutually implying each other—that is to say, the part played by automatism in the very *constitution* of the genuine (revolutionary) spirit. The spirit of resistance is no less authentic and alive because of this automatism; on the contrary, it comes to life with it. And it comes to life in a way that is surely not (or was surely not) without considerable consequences. Again: what is comic (and productive) is not simply the discrepancy between the spirit and the letter, their divergence, but also and above all their mutual implication. Or, I should perhaps say: the spirit emerging out of the very deficiencies of the letter. (In relation to this, and to Kleist's example, I should perhaps stress the virtue of assuming and tolerating the comedy when it comes to revolutionary enterprises, that is, the virtue of not succumbing to all-too-clever attitudes that ridicule the "pure coincidences" that can sometimes lead to revolutionary movements, as well as all the postures involved in collective enterprises, in their "blindly," automatically following and repeating, say, this or that "party line" or gesticulation.)

Let us now return to the example of imitation. The comic gesture involved in this procedure is in fact double: in the first step it makes us perceive a certain duality where we have so far perceived only a (more or less) harmonious One. It makes us perceive this duality simply by reproducing ("imitating") the One as faithfully as possible. This repetition/reproduction has the effect of introducing or "revealing" a gap in the original itself—a gap that we failed to notice before.

Since it would be rather difficult to quote (that is, reproduce) an example of comic imitation in a book, let me quote a verbal example that aims at the same effect: a brief but great comic exchange from the Marx Brothers' *A Night at the Opera*. After sitting with another woman for quite a while, Groucho (Driftwood) comes to Mrs. Claypool's table (she has been waiting for him all this time), and the following dialogue ensues:

DRIFTWOOD (Groucho):   That woman? Do you know why I sat with her?

MRS. CLAYPOOL (Margaret Dumont):   No—

DRIFTWOOD: Because she reminded me of you.

MRS. CLAYPOOL: Really?

DRIFTWOOD: Of course! That's why I'm sitting here with you. Because you remind me of you. Your eyes, your throat, your lips, everything about you reminds me of you, except you. How do you account for that?

If, then, the first step of the comic is this splitting divergence of the One—which produces the initial comic pleasure—what constitutes its second step? It consists simply in the comedy playing and constructing, from that point on, with this duality in a specific way: showing us the inner connections and mutual implications of the two elements of the duality. As I have already had occasion to point out, it is essential for comic suspense that the duality it produces remains an intrinsic duality of One—that is to say, that it does not simply fall apart into "two ones." Comedy is always a play with the inner ambiguity of the One. Comic duality is the inconsistency of the One (not simply its "composition").

In other words, if the trigger of the comic is a split, a break-up of an imaginary One (an image of One as wholeness, harmony, completeness, immediacy), this is by no means the whole comic story. True, One splits into two, yet the whole dynamism of comedy is related to the fact that these "two" (that we have only just come to see as two) betray a singular connection and unity, quite different from the unity of the One with which we started. The real comedy begins only when the limit the two elements represent to each other starts to function as their most intimate bond and the very territory of their encounter. And the initial problem is now reversed; a new impossibility comes to the fore: if the imaginary One encounters the impossibility of ever being a real, consistent One, the duality produced in the comic split encounters the impossibility of the two terms ever becoming completely independent, separate from each other (which is to say that it encounters a kind of insistence of the "one"). Does not one of the crucial dynamics of the comic consist precisely in the fact that the more the two terms push each in its own direction, the more violently one of the two will eventually pull the other with it? Not because they cannot exist one without the other, but because they are inherent to each other at some crucial point, because they are both generated by their common structural point in the first place. In other words, we are dealing not with the dialectics of "silence and cry" sustaining each other but, rather, with a dynamic of two cries, the common point of which—the Real that prevents them from becoming entirely separate—is silence. Good comedy, much as it indulges in shouting, never gives up on the point of this connective silence.

In relation to this question of an inherent link that makes it impossible for the comic two to become completely independent, I should stress the following point: it often happens that comic scenes are most literally constructed upon "the principle of elastic" or "the principle of the spring," that is to say, of a possible stretching and testing of its limit (the latter being precisely the point when, after some resistance, one of the two elements pulls the other over to its side). Bergson himself pointed to this mechanism when he introduced, to illustrate one of the elementary comic structures, the example of the jack-in-the-box.

> As children we have all played with the little man who springs out of his box. You squeeze him flat, he jumps up again. Push him lower, and he shoots up still higher. Crush him down beneath the lid, and often he will send everything flying. . . . It is a struggle between two stubborn elements, one of which, being simply mechanical, generally ends by giving in to the other, which treats it as a plaything. . . . Many a comic scene may indeed be referred to this simple type. For instance, in the scene of the *Mariage forcé* between Sganarelle and Pancrace, the entire *vis comica* lies in the conflict set up between the idea of Sganarelle, who wishes to make the philosopher listen to him, and the obstinacy of the philosopher, a regular talking-machine working automatically. As the scene progresses, the image of the Jack-in-the-box becomes more apparent, so that at last the characters themselves adopt its movements—Sganarelle pushing Pancrace, each time he shows himself, back into the wings, Pancrace returning to the stage after each repulse to continue his patter. And when Sganarelle finally drives Pancrace back and shuts him up inside the house—inside the box, one is tempted to say—a window suddenly flies open, and the head of the philosopher again appears as though it had burst open the lid of the box. (Bergson 1999, pp. 68–69)

This is indeed a good point and a good illustration of our thesis according to which comic duality is essentially an inconsistency of the One, displayed by comedy's simultaneous movement in two opposite directions: one splitting the One in two, the other not letting the two go completely separate ways. The quoted passage, however, is interesting not only because it convincingly draws our attention to this. Its interest also lies in the fact that Bergson, without being aware of it, indicates the limits of a crucial point of his theory, a deficiency in his own fundamental matrix of the comic at which I have already hinted.

When reading these lines from Bergson (and many others similar to them which abound in the *Essay*), the following question inevitably comes to mind: is this perseverance, this obstinacy with which something keeps returning and repeating, with which it resists all attempts at being eliminated and always finds a new window or a new "opening" through which it can peep out, not in fact very much akin to what Bergson calls "life impulse" or *élan vital*, opposing it to automatism and to the mechanical? Is it not only too clear from the description of the scene between Sganarelle and Pancrace that the movement, the dynamics, the life impulse are precisely on the side of the unstoppable "talking-machine" which refuses to shut up and cannot be locked up (inside the house or the box) for good? Why and in what sense would they rather belong to Sganarelle? Or, to take simply the elementary example of the jack-in-the-box (or any such spring toy) as "a struggle between two stubborn elements": are the motions of the one pushing the little man on the spring down, again and again, any less mechanical and repetitive than those of the little man himself? And do we not rather get the impression that the awkwardness and inelasticity are much more apparent in that "element" which, according to Bergson, is not mechanical, and that it is this "element" that tries to impose uniformity and stillness on what is going on?

The point, however, is not simply that in the given case Bergson should have reversed his matrix—that he failed to identify the two elements of his matrix correctly. The problem is more complex and more interesting. We could start to formulate it with the following questions. How is it that liveliness (or the impression of life) can emerge at the very core of the mechanical, and the mechanical at the very core of life? How can the mechanical itself function as belonging to an essential feature of ("organic") life itself: of its inner impulse or drive? Or of that "indestructibility of life" that is so often mentioned in relation to comedy? Another Bergsonian example of comic automatism is Harpagon's avarice (referring, of course, to Molière's comedy *The Miser*): a passion which, only just suppressed, automatically "turns on" again and again. Its automatic character is further accentuated by the repetition of certain phrases (like the famous "without dowry").

Yet it is more than obvious that Harpagon's avarice is not fascinating simply on account of its automatic, mechanical character, but rather because we can feel its all too lively pressure, which has the habit of always, even in the most impossible situations, finding a way of asserting itself. One could even say that the effect or impression of something mechanical (say, the repetition) follows from the fact that Harpagon's avarice is so alive and pressing that it turns all circumstances to its own advantage, to yet another opportunity of getting its own voice heard. In this perspective, it would seem that repetition is strictly speaking the effect of some liveliness which refuses to be "done in" and can in fact sometimes give the impression of using the whole person as a puppet through which (or at the expense of which) it will pursue its aims.

This perspective, however, would again be a simple reversal of Bergson's matrix or, more precisely, of its terms. Yet what I am trying to bring out is not that there is in fact a pure life vigor, a "basic instinct/drive" of life that keeps encountering different obstacles (conventions, morals, rules of conduct, expectations of others, and so on) that try to tame, suppress, and repress it, or to make it uniform. It is not that some lively and vivid spirit would constantly have to find its way around the dead letter which impedes it. What is at stake is that the spirit itself comes to life only with the (dead) letter, that vivacity as such emerges only with the repetition, and does not exist outside or prior to it. Were Harpagon not persistently *repeating* some of his actions and words, the effect of the *life impulse* of his miserly passion would fail to appear. Harpagon's avarice comes to life before our eyes as "drive" only because of, and through, its automatic repetition. Outside it, or in itself, it is nothing. It is only by this "mechanical" repetition that life can rise in front of us in all its vivacity, as well as produce the comic pleasure and the effect of "indestructibility" associated with comedy.

This is also how the comic can be a very good introduction to the psychoanalytic notion of the drive: the bottom line of both is that repetition is life—or, perhaps more precisely, that life is the inherent gap opened up by repetition itself, the gap existing at the very heart of repetition. This is also why, for Lacan, all drive (defined by him as "indestructible life") is ultimately a death drive—not because it aims at death, or "wants" it, but because it is life as driven by a dead letter. In this respect, and contrary to Bergson, the psychoanalytic perspective ultimately leads us to the following point: by objectifying this dead-letter-driven life itself, by producing it as an object (as comedy does), we do not mortify it even further, or glorify this mortification. Instead, we get a chance to break out of the mortifying spell of the latter. Yet this chance always passes by the letter itself.

STRUCTURAL DYNAMICS AND TEMPORALITY
OF THE COMICAL

And wit depends on dilatory time. . . .

—Shakespeare, *Othello*

In order to be able to better circumscribe the thing that distinguishes comedy from other, noncomical genres (tragedy or "serious drama," for example), we can perhaps start out from what is common to them.

What tragedy and comedy *do* have in common is that they are both based upon, and turn around, some fundamental discrepancy, incongruity, mismatch, discordance. For example: discrepancy between the intention behind an act and its actual effects, between desire and its satisfaction, between appearance and truth, and so on. In itself, the description of different forms that a discrepancy may assume does not take us very far along the path of understanding the functioning of comedy and tragedy, but we can detect an important difference between the two genres in terms of the way they come to structure this very field of incongruity. Hence it might not be completely idiotic to ask, for example, why it is that in tragedy misunderstandings are always tragic.

Tragedy structures the incongruity with the parameters and dialectics of desire. If we start on a fundamental level, the Lacanian conceptual deduction of this structure is well known and very helpful. It follows from the relationship between a demand (as articulated in the signifier) and its satisfaction: the latter is never "just right," it tends to involve a "too much" or "too little," a "too soon" or "too late.". . . Desire inhabits this difference or discrepancy; it is the very name for it. Tragedy is essentially the pain of this difference. It explores its scope, its space, and it explores it through the relation between the objective circumstances and the subjective singularity constitutive of the hero or the heroine.

Viewed from the perspective of tragedy, comedy tends to emerge as an utterly unrealistic, even fantasmatic, answer to the impasse involved in the relationship between desire and its satisfaction. In comedy, they say, things always add up to everybody's satisfaction. This view about everything adding up is quite persistent, although it is difficult to reconcile with the host of misencounters, misunderstandings, miscalculations, mistakes, misstatements, misrepresentations, misplacements, mismovements, misjudgments, misinterpretations, misdoings, misconducts, and misfirings on which comedy thrives. One usually pushes all these aside simply by saying that they are only temporary, and always lead to a final harmony and general satisfaction.

Against this view, several assertions must be made. The comic happy ending is not a sudden reversal of a previous misfortune or unhappiness, but is perfectly in line with the joyful satisfaction that lives all through the comedy, and is produced precisely by the mishaps listed above. Indeed—if anything, the comic happy ending, rather, comes with a certain amount of disappointment, since it implies the end of comedy and of its specific pleasure. In other words, comedy and comic satisfaction thrive on things that do not exactly add up. They thrive on these discrepancies as a source of pleasure rather than pain. Yet this by no means implies that comedy is distinguished from tragedy by what one would call today a "positive attitude," "positive thinking," the ability to find something positive and satisfactory even in the worst situations. Jumping to this conclusion would not only mean giving in to a gross ideologization of this question (the present social valuing and prizing of satisfaction and happiness plays an important role in assuring the current politicoeconomic hegemony, just as the valuing of self-sacrifice, renunciation, and pain has played a similar role in some past politicoeconomic configurations), but would also introduce a dimension of psychology that is utterly foreign to comedy. What is at stake in this difference between "tragic" and "comic" perspectives are not two ways of looking at the same configuration, one more negative and bitter, the other more positive and forthcoming. Instead, the "tragic" and the "comic" perspective spring from two different points inherent to the same configuration. Not only are they both true—they are both true because they are both "partial" and "partisan." They are not two views or perspectives on the same configuration, they are two views or perspectives *from* the same configuration (out). They do not look at the configuration of discrepancy, of antagonism, of conflicts and difficulties involved in the relationship between the demand and the satisfaction that answers this demand, they look *from this configuration out*, they are part of its antagonism. And it is not their attitude that determines what they see or, rather, what they show us, it is where they stand that determines their attitude.

Tragedy stands at the point of the demand, addressed to the Other; and from this point there is only one true way in which the discrepancy between this demand and the subsequent answer/satisfaction is articulated: as desire and its constitutive nonsatisfaction. We must be careful to understand this correctly. The fundamentally negative dimension of desire does not come from the fact that the satisfaction is always *less* than the desire, for it could very well be bigger, excessive. The point is that the excess reads negative because of the difference it implies in relation to the demand. Desire is the subjective figure of this difference as irreducible and irredeemable.

Comedy, on the other hand, stands at the point of the satisfaction; and from this point, there is also only one true way in which the discrepancy between this satisfaction and the demand that should correspond to it is articulated: as *jouissance*, enjoyment or "surplus-satisfaction." This is what interrupts the complementariness of demand and satisfaction from the point of view of satisfaction.

This difference in standpoint within a certain structural discrepancy also involves a shift in temporality, related to the question of how the dialectics of demand and satisfaction is affected by what comes first. Comedy switches the supposedly natural sequence, in which we start with the demand and end up with more or less inadequate satisfaction. The discrepancy that constitutes the motor of comedy lies not in the fact that satisfaction can never really meet demand, but rather that the demand can never really meet (some unexpectedly produced, surplus) satisfaction. This is not to say that, empirically or dramaturgically speaking, in comedy we cannot start with a demand. The point is that what comes as the answer to this demand, in all its disproportion, immediately introduces a surplus or a deviation that takes over the game and the initiative. In other words, in comedy it is not the satisfaction that runs after the demand, never able to fully catch up with it; it is, rather, that the satisfaction immediately overtakes the demand, so that the latter now has to stumble after satisfaction. Comedy or, more precisely, comic sequence is always inaugurated by some unexpected surplus-realization. This surplus-realization may well be produced by failure, by a mistake, an error, through misunderstanding (and it usually is), but the moment it occurs it changes the very structure of the field. The field of comedy is essentially a field in which the answer precedes the question, satisfaction precedes the demand. Not only do we (or the comic characters) not get what we asked for, on top of it (and not instead of it) we get something we haven't even asked for at all. And we have to cope with this surprising surplus, respond to it (this is the imperative of the genre). It is this discrepancy of something *en plus* that leads the way and drives the comedy.

The elementary form of the emergence of a surprising element of surplus-satisfaction/realization (or of a surplus-sense) could be discerned already in the phenomenon of jokes. In his discussion of jokes, Freud put forward the notion of an "incentive bonus,"[4] which could be defined as an unexpected supplement of pleasure that allows the release of more pleasure. Lacan also made this point quite directly: "*Witz* restores to the essentially unsatisfied demand its *jouissance*, and it does so in double (although identical) aspect of surprise and pleasure—the pleasure in surprise and the surprise in pleasure" (Lacan 1998, p. 121). The whole joke of jokes, if I might put it that way, lies in the fact that— much to everybody's surprise—the demand manages to find an unexpected satisfaction. The discrepancy at stake could also be formulated in topological instead of temporal terms: the satisfaction is produced somewhere else than where we expect it or await it. This is why the narrative of a joke does not simply prepare the setting for its final point, but also and above all directs and engages our attention elsewhere than where the point of the joke will pass. This is indeed a mechanism that we can observe in many jokes, and the following example illustrates it very clearly.

A man comes home from an exhausting day at work, plops down on the couch in front of the television, and tells his wife, "Get me a beer before it starts."

The wife sighs and gets him a beer. Fifteen minutes later, he says, "Get me another beer before it starts." She looks cross, but fetches another beer and slams it down next to him. He finishes that beer and a few minutes later says, "Quick, get me another beer, it's going to start any minute."

The wife is furious. She yells at him, "Is that all you're going to do tonight? Drink beer and sit in front of that TV? You're nothing but a lazy, drunken, fat slob, and furthermore. . . ."

The man sighs and says, "It's started. . . ."

While drawing our attention to the television set and making us expect the Thing to come from there (to "start" there), the narrative of the joke leads us away from the actual direction from which the blow comes, accentuating the effect of surprise. No joke succeeds without this element of surprise. Something else can be observed in this joke, something that could shed some light on the specific temporal modality of jokes: the point, "the joke of the joke," operates through the mechanism of what Lacan calls *le point de capiton*, the "quilting point"—that is to say, as the point at which an intervention of a Master-Signifier (in our case the final sentence, "It's started . . .") retroactively fixes the sense of the previous signifying elements, puts them in a new, unexpected, surprising perspective. In this way, we get a completely different story out of the same elements. If we think about it, we can see that this is the minimal mechanism at work in most jokes, usually described as "sense in nonsense" or as "production of an unexpected sense."

At this point we could perhaps draw a parallel between jokes and love encounters: could we not say that the love encounter is structured like a good joke? It always involves a dimension of an unexpected and surprising satisfaction, satisfaction of some other demand than the ones we have already had the opportunity to formulate. That is to say: we can very well set off on a date with the explicit intention of finding ourselves a "partner," or even falling in love. Yet if this happens, if something like a genuine love encounter takes place, it still always surprises us, since it necessarily takes place "elsewhere" than where we expected it, or intended it to take place; it takes place, so to speak, along "other lines." We look in one direction and it comes from the other, and it satisfies something in ourselves that we didn't even demand to be satisfied. This is why a love encounter can be quite upsetting, and is never simply a moment of pure happiness (where everything finally "adds up"). It is always accompanied by a feeling of perplexity, confusion, a feeling that we've got something that we don't know exactly what to do with, and yet something rather pleasant. Two kinds of reaction can follow from this: we can take the ball from there, so to speak, and play on, or else we can react by trying to found this love by retrospectively formulating the demand to which this surprisingly produced satisfaction was supposed to reply. And this is where the tricky part of love begins, for we can get stuck here. The supplement of pleasure, instead of allowing the release or production of more pleasure, could be retroactively transformed from supplement to complement. That is to say: every love encounter brings with it the temptation to reinscribe the surprising, accidental and bonus-like dimension of the satisfaction into the linear or circular coupling of demand and (its) satisfaction or, in other terms, of desire and *jouissance*. This is the temptation to recognize the other (that we encountered through this surprising emergence of a bonus satisfaction) as the answer to all our prayers, that is, as an answer to our (previously existing) demand. This understandable and seemingly innocent, even charming, move can, however, have rather catastrophic consequences. It immediately disavows the very element of discontinuity that is crucial in any love encounter. It immediately closes the accidentally produced way out of the impossibility involved in the relation between demand and its satisfaction, and it closes it precisely by transforming this impossibility into a possibility. In this move, the love encounter is reconfigured in terms of an emphatic moment of a perfect complementariness of demand and satisfaction, and glorified as a case when the satisfaction did in fact meet our demand. In this way love is locked up in the eternal past, it can be lived only as a nostalgic memory.

I should therefore stress that the funny (as well as the subversive) side of a love encounter lies precisely in the fact that the other (that we encounter) is an answer to *none* of our prayers and dreams but, rather, the bearer of an unexpected surplus-element that we might only get the chance to dream about in what follows. If we lose sight of the fact that in a genuine love encounter we get something that we haven't exactly asked for, then we lose the perspective of love, in both meanings of the word. What happens in a love encounter is not simply that the sexual nonrelation is momentarily suspended with an unexpected emergence of a (possible) relation, but something rather more complex: it is that the nonrelation itself suddenly emerges as a mode (as well as the condition) of a relation. A "happy" love encounter is the nonrelation at its purest or, perhaps more precisely, it is a nonrelation as redoubled. As in comedy, not only do we not get what we asked for, on top of that (and not instead) we get something we haven't even asked for. The nonrelation is supplemented by another nonrelation, which can then use the thing that obstructs the relation as its very condition (and can function like the Freudian "incentive bonus").

This brings us to the next suggestion. If a love encounter is like a good joke, then what is love in its duration and temporality— what is, as we say, a love that lasts? One could reply that love is structured like comedy, with its specific temporality, which I will discuss below. As such, it could be defined as *a nonrelation that lasts.* Comedy is the genre that uses the supplementary nonrelation as the condition of a relation. I shall not pursue this structural affinity between love and comedy any further here,[5] but let me just stress that it is conceptually very useful, since it can help us to think of love in terms different from the two predominant discourses on love: that of all-consuming *amour-passion*, which is presented as a flame that fuses the two lovers in one; and that of the ideal (prevailing today) of two autonomous and independent *egos* constructing a "meaningful" relationship, based on mutual recognition, respect, and exchange. There is a certain affinity between love and comedy which has to do with the way they are organized around a central object which incarnates the very impossibility of any smooth complementariness of the elements involved. This object functions as the obstacle that paradoxically enables the (comic or loving) two to relate to each other. Remove this obstacle, and their "relationship" will fall apart. This is not the (in)-famous obstacle that enables us to desire the other in her very inaccessibility; on the contrary, it is an obstacle that gives us the access to the other in her very materiality, so to speak.

We should now take a closer look at the difference between the structure and the dynamics of jokes on the one hand, and of comedy on the other. This difference concerns above all the temporality involved in their respective processes, which then affects the destiny of that surprising object-sense that is produced in them.

Unlike the temporal structure of comedy, a joke is always situated (exclusively) in the instantaneity of the moment at which its point passes. The pleasure in jokes is instantaneous and very much confined as to its time, which does not mean, however, that it cannot be repeated. If we pass the joke on, it will again produce satisfaction. The repeating or passing on of jokes is part of the pleasure we take in them, and in this sense we could say that jokes are by definition a promiscuous way of finding pleasure; there is something Don Juanesque in them. We can find pleasure in the same joke only if we change partners. Comic pleasure is different in its temporality: it is not instantaneous, but stretches over a certain lapse of time.

What is at stake, however, is not simply a question of how long something lasts; there are very long jokes and very short comic sequences (gags). The difference in temporality concerns the temporality of pleasure (or satisfaction): a joke is always *final*, it always comes at the end, which is thus also true for the pleasure/satisfaction produced by jokes. *At the end,* we are left with a certain amount of satisfaction, and what precedes it (the narrative of the joke) is a preparatory phase leading to and making the final "joke" possible. Comic sequences are not constructed in this manner. Satisfaction usually arises at the very beginning; instead of closing a comic sequence it inaugurates it, it opens it up and is then kept alive (with fluctuations which follow a certain rhythm) during the whole sequence. Satisfaction does not conclude the game (as it does in the case of jokes), it launches it. Jokes produce all kinds of surprising object-senses, and when they do so, they leave them to hang in the air and slowly die away. Between one joke and another there might be all sorts of resemblances (in their technique or their object), but there is also a radical discontinuity: we always start anew, building a new story from scratch. A comic sequence, on the other hand, does not leave the surprising, erratic object-sense to die away in the air; rather, it picks it up as a new starting point, a new cue to build with. In this respect, comedy is a paradoxical continuity that builds, constructs (almost exclusively) with discontinuity; discontinuity (the erratic object-sense) is the very stuff of comic continuity. Comedy has a marvelous way of starting on one track and continuing on the other, as if this were completely natural.

Let us simply take an example here, a piece of comic dialogue which was circulating on the Internet a few years ago.

Hu's on First
by James Sherman

(We take you now to the Oval Office.)

GEORGE: Condi! Nice to see you. What's happening?

CONDI: Sir, I have the report here about the new leader of China.

GEORGE: Great. Lay it on me.

CONDI: Hu is the new leader of China.

GEORGE: That's what I want to know.

CONDI: That's what I'm telling you.

GEORGE: That's what I'm asking you. Who is the new leader of China?

CONDI: Yes.

GEORGE: I mean the fellow's name.

CONDI: Hu.

GEORGE: The guy in China.

CONDI: Hu.

GEORGE: The new leader of China.

CONDI: Hu.

GEORGE: The Chinaman!

CONDI: Hu is leading China.

GEORGE: Now whadd'ya asking me for?

CONDI: I'm telling you Hu is leading China.

GEORGE: Well, I'm asking you. Who is leading China?

CONDI: That's the man's name.

GEORGE: That's whose name?

CONDI: Yes.

GEORGE: Will you or will you not tell me the name of the new leader of China?

CONDI: Yes, sir.

GEORGE: Yassir? Yassir Arafat is in China? I thought he was in the Middle East.

CONDI: That's correct.

GEORGE: Then who is in China?

CONDI: Yes, sir.

GEORGE: Yassir is in China?

CONDI: No, sir.

GEORGE: Then who is?

CONDI: Yes, sir.

GEORGE: Yassir?

CONDI: No, sir.

GEORGE: Look, Condi. I need to know the name of the new leader of China. Get me the Secretary-General of the U.N. on the phone.

CONDI: Kofi?

GEORGE: No, thanks.

CONDI: You want Kofi?

GEORGE: No.

CONDI: You don't want Kofi.

GEORGE: No. But now that you mention it, I could use a glass of milk. And then get me the U.N.

CONDI: Yes, sir.

GEORGE: Not Yassir! The guy at the U.N.

CONDI: Kofi?

GEORGE: Milk! Will you please make the call?

CONDI: And call who?

GEORGE: Who is the guy at the U.N.?

CONDI: Hu is the guy in China.

GEORGE: Will you stay out of China?!

CONDI: Yes, sir.

GEORGE: And stay out of the Middle East! Just get me the guy at the U.N.

CONDI: Kofi.

GEORGE: All right! With cream and two sugars. Now get on the phone.

(Condi picks up the phone.)

CONDI: Rice here.

GEORGE: Rice? Good idea. And a couple of egg rolls, too. Maybe we should send some to the guy in China. And the Middle East. Can you get Chinese food in the Middle East?

If we compare this example of comic dialogue with an example of a joke (for instance, the one above), the following temporal and dynamic difference is evident. In jokes, the sparkle (of surprise and satisfaction) is produced at the end, and the narrative leading to it is a construction that makes this final sparkle possible. In comedy, there is first an unexpected sparkle (a kind of inaugural joke), and the unexpected surplus it produces is not conclusive, but functions as the motor of the subsequent comic sequence. One could also say that the inaugural surplus introduces a fundamental discrepancy that drives comedy further and further, and it is this surplus/discrepancy itself that serves as the "glue" of the comic events.

In our example it all starts with the emergence of a first comic *point de capiton*, resulting from the homonymy between the name of the Chinese leader (Hu) and the question "who?" Yet this "quilting point" is itself treated as a comic object, stretched in both directions, until it produces—in this process of stretching—a new "quilting point," the homonymy between "Yes, sir" and Yassir. Thus introduced is the second object of comic stretching, which continues besides, as well as with the help of the first one, until a third pops up: Kofi (Annan) as coffee. Now we already have three comic objects in the air, soon to be joined by the fourth: Miss Rice in the form of rice. It is clear that in principle this could go on forever, and that what I propose to call a comic sequence is not conclusive in itself, that is to say, it does not carry in itself its own logical or necessary conclusion. This in no way contradicts the fact that one of the main skills of the mastery of comedy is to know when to stop, and how to do it with as much comic style as possible.

This functioning of comedy (despite the numerous "quilting points" that it might produce in its process) could also be related to what looks like its miraculous fluidity. It helps us to see more clearly how comic fluidity is always a kind of *staccato* fluidity, so to speak. The art of comedy is precisely a singular continuity-through-interruption, a continuity that, as I have already stressed, builds with—and is built through—interruptions and breaks, a continuity that constructs with discontinuity, a continuity whose very stuff is a discontinuity. It is precisely in this respect that the question of the comic object comes to the fore: the question of the disruptive surplus generated by and through the comic movement, yet at the same time influencing this very movement that generates it, functioning as its cause or drive. In this sense, the comic object is at the same time the effect and the cause of the comic movement; it is the point in which the disruptive, loose-end surplus that breaks the fluid chain of the action also starts to function as that which allows the comic movement to move on, to continue (in what might be an unexpected direction). In other words, the comic object incarnates the very point of the continuous discontinuity.

Let us set these differences between the functioning of jokes and that of comedy against the following schema:

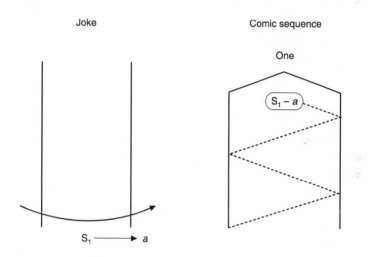

In the case of jokes, we start with two signifying series. In the example quoted earlier, the first one turns around the fact that something "is about to start," the second around the usual domestic quarrels. We "spontaneously" perceive a certain relation between them, its meaning being more or less what comes out in the wife's outburst just before the end ("Is that all you're going to do tonight? Drink beer and sit in front of that TV? You're nothing but a lazy, drunken, fat slob, and furthermore . . ."). Then comes the punch line, the joke's joke, the "quilting point" ("It's started . . ."—S_1 on our schema), which retroactively changes the spontaneously perceived meaning of the whole story by showing how one of the two series has always-already been inscribed in the other: "something is about to start" refers not to something that will "start" on TV, but to the domestic quarrel itself. The cause of the fight is the (anticipated) fight itself; the cause already presupposes the effect. The supposed linearity and necessity of the constitution of meaning are broken; out comes its contingency and retroactive constitution.

I am tempted to use this as a cue for a brief digression on the question of what exactly we laugh at when we laugh at jokes. There is a level where we clearly laugh at the joke's butt, at persons(s) or thing(s) that the joke makes fun of. Yet this is not the only level on which a joke functions. There is also the fact that each and every concrete joke (about this or that person or situation) is also a joke about the very functioning of our symbolic universe as constituted through signifiers and their specific, counterintuitive way of making sense. In other words, besides its story—and by the very "technical" means of constructing this story—a joke also brings to the fore something in which we are embedded deeply and permanently, without necessarily being aware of its functioning: the paradoxical, "illogical," nonlinear and precarious constitution of our (symbolic) universe through speech. This, I believe, is what Lacan has in mind with the following remark concerning Freud's work on jokes:

> All that Freud develops from there on consists in demonstrating the annihilating, the truly destroying, and disruptive character of the signifying game in relation to what we might call the existence of the real. In playing with the signifier man brings into question, at any moment, his world, all the way to its very roots. The value of the joke . . . is its possibility to play on the fundamental non-sense of all usage of sense. It is possible, at any moment, to bring into question all sense, as far as the latter is based on the usage of the signifier. As a matter of fact, this usage is itself profoundly paradoxical in relation to every possible signification, since it is this usage itself that creates that what it will have to support. (Lacan 1994, p. 294)

There is a paradoxical way of functioning of sense that we become aware of only when a sense surprises us. We could thus say that beside their particular content, jokes also always remind us of this or that (unperceived in the routine) peculiarity of the signifying order that constitutes our world, and that we also laugh at this. On a certain level, there is a dimension of precariousness and fundamental uncertainty in our very world that gets articulated and becomes manifest in every joke. In this perspective, the process of joking is not only "work done with the help of the Symbolic" (condensations, displacements, playing with homonyms, and so on), but always also something that displays the "Symbolic at work." This implies that when we laugh at a joke, we laugh not only at what it produces as its more or less witty point, but also at the fact that it produces something to begin with, and at how it produces it. In other words, the so-called joke technique is not only a means of constructing a joke, but is itself also the object of the joke it tells, its butt. What is funny at this level is the very possibility and functioning of all these condensations, displacements, of nonsense making perfect sense, and vice versa. . . .

If, as suggested above, there is a dimension of precariousness and fundamental uncertainty in our very world that gets articulated and becomes manifest in every joke, the question arises: How come we actually laugh at this? Should it not, rather, cause in us something like existential anxiety? In answer to this question, I am tempted to propose the following hypothesis: just as the narrative of the joke diverts our attention from the point where its twist will take place, the content-related butt of the joke diverts our attention from this other, more radical and more discomforting butt. Or, in other words: when we laugh at the butt, a certain amount of pleasure gets realized and makes it possible for us to laugh also in face of this discomforting dimension (displaying the precariousness of our world and its dependence on contingent mechanisms of the production of sense), instead of being seized by anxiety in the face of it.

If we were to accept this hypothesis, we would have to supplement Freud's theory of jokes with a mechanism that operates in the opposite direction from the one he established. According to

Freud, the joke technique (puns, condensations, displacements . . .) produces a certain amount of preliminary pleasure ("fore-pleasure"), which is "pure" in the sense that it is not related to any content of the joke. This fore-pleasure has a similar "toxic" effect to, say, a drink or two: it lowers our inhibitions, and thus allows us to laughingly accept the tendency (aggressiveness, sexuality) that appears at the level of the joke's content and which we would refuse, even turn away from in disgust, if it appeared outside the context of the joke (Freud 1976, p. 202). In other words, the joke work or joke technique produces a preliminary pleasure which helps us to overcome certain cultural inhibitions and accept certain problematic contents (like open sexuality or aggressiveness), and when this takes place, the principal quota of pleasure is discharged—namely, the energy previously used to maintain these inhibitions. The main stream of laughter, so to speak, in tendentious jokes is thus related to this momentary lifting of certain inhibitions (ibid., pp. 143–145).

Should we not take a step further here, however, and ask—in relation to the previous discussion—to what extent the libidinal tendentiousness of jokes (like their sexual and aggressive contents) are not already themselves a kind of smokescreen? A smokescreen that makes it possible for us to confront universal nonsense as the presupposition of all sense in a way that is not direct, but goes through the intermediary of the joke's content or butt that we laugh at? In this perspective, one would have to accept the possibility that the pleasure in obscenity and aggression, culturally admitted in the form or context of a joke, could itself have the effect of "lowering inhibitions" and making us more tolerant in accepting the real, paradoxical, and contingent constitution of our world, as well as its precariousness. A (tendentious) joke would thus not only be a way of uttering obscene or in some other way indecent truths with the help of different techniques of playing with the signifier and its ambiguities, but would also be, and to the same extent, the uttering of truth about a fundamental ambiguity of our world with the help of different content-related indecencies. To put it more precisely: these two dimensions (and directions) could in fact be said to exist in a circular relationship of mutual implication, in which they presuppose and enable each other, so that it is strictly impossible to unknot them into a linear explanation of the causality of jokes.

The point of their intersection, the point where the two dimensions imply each other, is the point marked on our schema by the (Lacanian) symbol a, the surplus-satisfaction as object that results from the signifying operation of S_1, the corporeal dimension of the signifier existing, in the case of jokes, in the form of laughter. We must not forget that the success of the signifying operation, the triumph of the new Master-Signifier produced by the joke, is strictly dependent on this corporeal effect/dimension.

Let us now look at the right side our schema, showing the functioning of a comic sequence in its difference from the functioning of jokes. (I use the term "comic sequence" to designate the central modality of comic structure, since the term comedy implies a larger field—as a genre designation of a play or a movie it refers to its entire composition, which might also involve other things besides comic sequences—lyric sequences, neutral sequences, jokes. . . .) The upper part of the schema indicates the first step of the comical, the split of an (imaginary, "obvious") Unity or One. This split may be induced by different comic techniques: by an immediate introduction of a surplus-object that sticks to the One and indicates its division, by different modes of redoubling and/or repetition. . . . A comic sequence could also be inaugurated by something quite similar to a joke. This is the case in our own example of comic dialogue. The first misunderstanding (the confusion between the name Hu and the question who?) is actually a joke—perhaps not a hilarious one, but a joke nevertheless. Up to this point—

GEORGE: Condi! Nice to see you. What's happening?

CONDI: Sir, I have the report here about the new leader of China.

GEORGE: Great. Lay it on me.

CONDI: Hu is the new leader of China.

GEORGE: That's what I want to know.

—the comic piece is in fact a joke. In Bush's referential and signi-fying universe, Hu becomes *who*. He is the butt of the joke, which is telling us that the President of the USA has no clue whatsoever about what is going on in China, or its politics. The reversal of Hu into "who" is the "quilting point" of the two signifying series, which become apparent as two precisely in this turn, through this quilting point.—As a matter of fact, I should add an important point to my description of the functioning of jokes: the two series designated in the schema might not be so obvious from the out-set, and they usually aren't. It is the final point, the *point de capiton*, which *at the same time* reveals a duality or split in what might have previously seemed to be a homogeneous narrative, and produces a short circuit between the two series. In other words, our schema of the functioning of jokes should not be read as showing a tem-poral unfolding of a joke (top-down). What was said about the fundamental temporality of a joke as being that of an *instant* (in which its point passes) affects its entire structure. Our schema is thus drawn strictly from the point of view of the moment at which the *point de capiton* appears and captures the structure of the joke as made apparent at that moment. The other schema, however, that of the comic sequence, can be read as structuring a certain length of time and displaying an elementary form of its unfolding. We have seen how this unfolding can be inaugurated by, among other things, a joke. Yet when a joke appears as a constitutive part of a comic sequence, its destiny is different from its usual destiny. This is very clear in our example, and can be less clear in some others, but I must insist that this structure is at work in all comic se-quences. In our example we can clearly observe how the Master-Signifier produced by the inaugural joke (*who* that replaces Hu) does not simply triumph and carry away its signifying victory. It is immediately reversed by a reaffirmation of Hu ("Hu is the new leader of China."—"That's what I want to know."—"That's what I'm telling you,"), only for the latter to be reversed again, and then have its next triumphant comeback ("That's what I'm asking you. Who is the new leader of China?"—"Yes."). In this exchange we can observe how a Master-Signifier that pops up in comic sequences is immediately transformed into a comic object that both protagonists try to appropriate for themselves. It becomes an object of stretching and of other different manipulations which constitute the comedy of the sequence, and also gradually bring in new Master-Signifiers as comic objects ("Yes, sir"—"Yassir"; "Kofi"—"Coffee"; "Rice"—"rice"). We could also describe what is going on here in the following way: the *suture* as the effect of the Master-Signifier is transformed by comedy into something like an elastic band, the stretching of which opens up the comic space (and defines its extension), whereas the Master-Signifier itself is transformed into a comic object, an object-like entity as a compound of enjoyment and of sense (Lacan would say *jouis-sense*, which was translated into English as "enjoy-meant"). This is what appears in our schema as $S_1 — a$. This is the "ball" that bounces back and forth in the comic space, as in table tennis ("ping-pong"), and also usually involves a snowball effect, increasing its comic potential and effect as it continues on its way.

It is very important for the construction of a comic sequence that the signifying objects produced in it, including the comic pleasure that sticks to them, are used as the material and the means of its further construction, not simply released as such. Some could be released as jokes or gags that remain just that, but most have to be kept within the comic field and used as possible passages to further events with which to construct the comic sequence. This is why a series of consecutive jokes and gags, with no inner connection, is not enough to qualify as comedy—it does not fulfill one of the crucial conditions of comedy, which I have described as continuity that constructs with discontinuity.

REPETITION

> Hegel remarks somewhere that all facts and personages of great im-
> portance in world history occur, as it were, twice. He forgot to add:
> the first time as tragedy, the second as farce.

This famous line with which Marx begins *The Eighteenth Brumaire of Louis Bonaparte* is a very appropriate starting point for the reflections on which we are about to embark in this chapter, combining two principal themes: philosophical or, largely, conceptual questions involved in the notion of repetition; and the question of comedy ("farce").

Comedy's affinity for repetition is a well-established fact, and repetition is among the most prominent comic techniques. There might, however, exist a deeper affinity than a merely technical one (or one could also say: a technique is never a "mere technique"). As the other side of repetition as technique there exists— or so I shall try to argue—repetition as *constitutive* of the comic genre as such. And it is on account of this that comedy is not simply an anecdotic problem of philosophy, but also an immanently philosophical problem. In order to work our way through to this point, we shall start out from some philosophical issues involved in repetition.

It might not be too much of an exaggeration to claim that the discovery of repetition, or of a specific dimension of repetition, is the Event that inaugurates so-called contemporary philosophy and gives a meaning to this designation. There is Marx and *The Eighteenth Brumaire*; then there are of course Nietzsche, Kierkegaard, and Freud, all of whom turned to the concept of repetition in order to work out some crucial aspect of their thought. And then there is Lacan's return to Freud, in which he promotes repetition in one of the "four fundamental concepts of psychoanalysis" (in his 1964 seminar); and there is, of course, Deleuze and his "return to Nietzsche," so to speak, in what could be called his most monumental and philosophically intriguing work, *Difference and Repetition* (first published in France in 1968).

There are, of course, important, even irreconcilable, differences between these projects, but there is also one important point that they all share: repetition is viewed, posited, elaborated as fundamentally different from the logic of representation. In Deleuze, this takes the form of a straightforward conceptual war: repetition against representation. Psychoanalysis, on the other hand, has never quite dismissed the theme of representation—it has, rather, further elaborated it, and in a surprising direction. Yet it also clearly pointed out its limit, in practice as well as in theory: Freud soon discovered that there is a limit to what remembering and interpretation (which he first posited as the principal tools of psychoanalysis) can accomplish in analysis. They can work most of the time, yet there are certain points that can be approached, and worked through, only via repetition.

BETWEEN TRAGEDY AND FARCE

Marx's considerations in *The Eighteenth Brumaire* are not a bad way to enter the conceptual complexities of the notion of repetition. Although Marx does not offer anything like a theory of repetition, his remarks have a way of enumerating some of the crucial points involved in this theme. In what follows the opening remark on Hegel and repetition, Marx's elaborations bring forward three different elements. On the one hand we have two types of repetition (only one of which is "farce") and, on the other, a radical break with repetition, yet a break that paradoxically throws us into a kind of pure compulsion to repeat.

Marx's main concern in *The Eighteenth Brumaire*, of course, is not the relationship between repetition and farce but the question whether, and to what extent, a repetition is also a place or a bearer of something new—that is to say, to what extent it can constitute a break (with the given, or with the past). Thus we have, on the one side, revolutionary periods that "conjure up the spirits of the past to their service and borrow from them names, battle cries and costumes in order to present the new scene of world history in this time-honoured disguise and this borrowed language" (Marx 1967, p. 10). Repetition of old names, battle cries, and costumes can be a way through which something new gets constituted. In Alain Badiou's terms, one could say that this is a repetition of the "trace of the event" which "resurrects" its emancipatory power in the new circumstances.[6] Here, repetition is in the service of the new; resurrection of the dead, as Marx puts it, serves the purpose "of finding once more the spirit of revolution, not of making its ghost walk about again." On the other side, there are also empty repetitions, described in the last part of the quote, repetitions as "ghosts" (and "farces"), the prototype of which is the February Revolution and its aftermath: "From 1848 to 1851 only the ghost of the old revolution walked about . . ." (ibid., p. 12). The bourgeois revolution, the rising of Napoleon's nephew (Louis), the "Second Republic"—this is where Marx sees repetition as farce, as conjuring up ghosts.

From this rapid summary it is already clear that what is involved in the issue of farce is not simply the relationship between a first apparition (as the original) and its repetition but, rather, the relationship between two types of repetition and the possible originality they imply. When we are dealing, to put it bluntly, with a "good" repetition, the old form is repeated in the function of producing something new. This is what is lacking in "bad repetitions" (such as the February Revolution). And not only do the latter fail to produce anything new, they use the very form of the new, that is, the form of revolution, only the better to perpetuate the same fundamental bourgeois content. The bourgeoisie arose from revolution (which was a "genuine revolution"—in the sense that it involved a real modification of social relationships), and at the same time it needs revolution (this time an "empty" one) as the form of its perpetuation; the bourgeois order exists through its perpetual revolutionizing.[7]

Considering how, in the Marxist tradition, the notion of revolution is inseparably bound to the notion of the proletariat, it is most interesting to reread these pages of The Eighteenth Brumaire, which make of revolution a preeminently bourgeois form: the bourgeoisie was born with revolution and it needed, for its further development, new and newer revolutions. Characteristic of these bourgeois revolutions, according to Marx, is a spectacular and frenetic activity:

> Bourgeois revolutions, like those of the eighteenth century, storm swiftly from success to success; their dramatic effects outdo each other; men and things seem set in sparkling brilliants; ecstasy is the everyday spirit; but they are short-lived; soon they have attained their zenith, and a long crapulent depression lays hold of society before it learns soberly to assimilate the results of its storm-and-stress period. (Marx 1967, pp. 13–14)

To this, Marx opposes proletarian revolutions as revolutions of the future—not only or simply in the temporal sense of the term, but also and above all structurally: that is to say, proletarian revolutions are supposed to break radically with the very logic of the repetition of the past for the purposes of the present (or in the interests of the future). Marx's wager is thus a revolution that cannot/should not be a repetition. To quote the famous passage:

> The social revolution of the nineteenth century cannot draw its poetry from the past, but only from the future. It cannot begin with itself before it has stripped off all superstition in regard to the past. Earlier revolutions required recollections of past world history in order to drug themselves concerning their own content. In order to arrive at its own content, the revolution of the nineteenth century must let the dead bury their dead. (ibid., pp. 12–13)

For the new revolution, repetition can no longer be a way through which it could realize its novelty, its break (with the given), the difference it brings to the world. It cannot dress up in the old costumes and repeat past phrases in order to carry out "the task of its time" (as the old French Revolution did—"in Roman costumes and with Roman phrases").[8] The new revolution will break, once and for all, the circle of historical repetition.

However, the *reality* of proletarian revolutions, as described by Marx, is quite different. For it rather seems that with them repetition runs amok, as is clear from our last quote from *The Eighteenth Brumaire*:

> On the other hand, proletarian revolutions, like those of the nineteenth century, criticise themselves constantly, interrupt themselves continually in their own course, come back to the apparently accomplished in order to begin at afresh, deride with unmerciful thoroughness the inadequacies, weaknesses and paltrinesses of their first attempts, seem to throw down their adversary only in order that he may draw new strength from the earth and rise again, more gigantic, before them. . . . (ibid., p. 14)

Here we come across some paradoxical necessity to repeat, to restart again and again, as if the imperative of breaking with repetition ("let the dead bury their dead") only really brought us to repetition in its pure form, as if it were only "beyond repetition" (as repetition of the past phrases) that we arrive at the very quintessence of repetition, that is, at repetition that repeats (and thus differentiates) *itself*. Although it is only indirectly sketched out in Marx's text, the logic of this passage from the "repetition of the necessary" to the "necessity of repetition," from the necessity of what is repeated to repetition as necessity, describes an important aspect of what happened to the theme of repetition in the post-Hegelian part of the nineteenth century, when this theme not only moves to the foreground, but also first rises as an independent conceptual issue. This is also true of some other elements that we touched upon in this brief overview of *The Eighteenth Brumaire*, such as the question of the different modes of repetition and the question of repetition in relation to the new, as we shall see in what follows.

But before we leave Marx, there is one more point to be made in relation to the last quote. What we can see emerging in the repetition it describes (with the revolution's seemingly vain attempts against an infinitely bigger adversary) is also a specific comic dimension, quite different from the one that Marx refers to as "farce." It is not an "empty repetition" as revolution in the service of perpetuating the given, but a stubborn attempt to do something against all odds, which, because of its repetitious character, leaves the realm of the heroic and enters a territory closer to the comic— not because it keeps failing, but because it keeps insisting.

CONCEPTUAL STAKES OF REPETITION: DELEUZE AND LACAN

At this point, I will take the opportunity to embark on what might seem like a considerable digression into purely conceptual (philosophical and psychoanalytic) issues of repetition, which have little to do with comedy. If this might seem like a considerable digression, it is because . . . it is a considerable digression. We will be talking about repetition "in itself and for itself," focusing on how its conceptual stakes are articulated by two prominent contemporary thinkers, Deleuze and Lacan. To those who might lack the interest in this "purely philosophical" debate of repetition, I can at least promise that it will eventually bring us back to a very important dimension of comedy.

Let us start with Deleuze and his *Difference and Repetition*. The title itself is very eloquent: not "Being and Time," not "Being and Nothingness," not perhaps "Being and Event," but "Difference and Repetition"—whereby the shift, the mutation of Being into Difference, is by no means accidental. For the central point of Deleuze's book could be summarized in these two theses:

(1) Being, the only (and univocal) Being, is Difference.
(2) The only real access to Being–Difference is repetition (as opposed to representation).

The simplest way to elaborate these two highly condensed propositions a little might be to do it from the perspective of Deleuze's relationship to Kierkegaard and his notion of repetition. For Deleuze starts out with a distinctly Kierkegaardian emphasis, but he then develops his project at a certain distance from Kierkegaard (and in an acclaimed proximity to Nietzsche).

Reduced to its elementary framework, the Kierkegaardian conception of repetition is divided into two levels. The first level could be summed up with the thesis *There is no repetition* (Kierkegaard's hero, who embarks on the path of attempted repetition, stumbles, at every step, against its radical impossibility), and its materialistic turn, also formulated by Kierkegaard himself: *What is repeated is the very impossibility of repetition.* This constitutes the first level. The second level is related to what Kierkegaard pictures on the horizon, namely Repetition as essentially transcendent. There is hope for the repetition of the Moment (in its uniqueness, singularity, exceptionality), and this hope belongs to the third of the Kierkegaardian circles of the aesthetic, the ethical, and the religious. Repetition does not belong to the order of laws, be it natural, aesthetic, or ethical laws: it is strictly impossible under the law, and belongs to the register of miracle.

In relation to this outline of Kierkegaard's essay, Deleuze's position could be described as follows. Although he preserves the idea that repetition is foreign to any law, and belongs to the order of miracle,[9] he rejects the rest of Kierkegaard's second step (second level), on account of its appeal to the transcendent. Instead of this second level, Deleuze proposes a kind of (redoubled) affirmation of the first, seemingly negative one, an affirmation that will liberate what is always-already positive in the first level. That is to say: yes, it is true, what is repeated is the very impossibility of repetition, but instead of seeing this (through the prism of representation) as purely negative—as repetition motivated by failure and impossibility—we have to make another shift of perspective and, in this way, come to perceive that which nevertheless succeeds in getting repeated, which never stops being repeated or, one might also say, that which never succeeds in not being repeated: namely, difference. The only thing that gets repeated is difference itself. Difference is the positive, the excessive, of repetition's failure. In it, apparent failure turns out to be success. Hence Deleuze's further thesis: the motor, the driving force of repetition is not a failure, a lack, a deficiency, but a pure excessive positivity of the production of differences, which constitutes a sort of Deleuzian "primary process." Difference is excess that repeats itself. In this sense difference is not a secondary (albeit positive) product of failure but is, strictly speaking, primary; it is prior to failure, which has for its references identity or similarity, both of which exist only on the basis of difference and starting from difference.

Identity, similarity, sameness, one—these are all secondary categories which, according to Deleuze, do not enable us to think difference, but are themselves products of (the labor of) difference and of thinking difference, its effect. However, if identity, similarity, and sameness are neither the condition of the being of difference nor the condition of thinking difference, they are the condition of its representation. (Our) representation of difference necessarily proceeds from categories of identity, similarity, or sameness (and further convokes the operations of analogy and opposition); yet by offering a concept of difference (one could say: by producing difference as a conceptual object), it chases difference from the concept itself. The difference that corresponds to the mode of representation is always an external difference. On the level of representation, difference always appears as a difference between two entities or two identities, whereas Deleuze would like to get to the inner difference that precedes identity. And this is where the elaboration of repetition in all its radicalism leads.

According to Deleuze, this was Nietzsche's Copernican revolution, for this is how he reads Nietzsche's concept of the eternal return: difference does not revolve around and proceed from sameness; on the contrary, it is sameness that revolves around difference and proceeds from it as a secondary phenomenon. Repetition, however, does not fit this description (it is not the eternal return) already in itself and in its whole: repetition itself contains, or falls into, different moments through which it somehow abolishes its own "bad" dynamics and affirms the "good" one.

The dynamics and the logic of repetition is thus distinguished, in Deleuze, by three different moments of repetition, three temporalities of repetition, which are also three different types of repetition. These three moments correspond, on a much more developed and elaborated conceptual level, to the triple matrix discussed in relation to Marx. One is repetition in the temporal mode of "Before" (*Avant*), repetition in relation to the past, to something that has already been; it is a mechanical, stereotypical, "bare" (*nue*) repetition, which does not bring about anything new and does not change a thing. It operates by insufficiency or failure (*par défaut*). A subject is confronted with this repetition when an action is absolutely too big for her. The second repetition is a repetition that always appears in some disguise; its temporal mode is that of "During" (*Pendant*), and it is a repetition that introduces a change (a metamorphosis) into the world. Here, the subject becomes equal to her act and to the metamorphosis it implies. The third repetition implies the mode of the Future, of what is (yet) to come (*Avenir*). In this singular mode the repetition separates what was created (in the second mode), the product, from its conditions and its genesis, and affirms this product as unconditional and beyond any kind of subject, as an absolutely independent entity, which is the embodiment of the novelty of repetition, of repetition as novelty.

Deleuze qualifies the first moment as the moment of comedy and the second as that of tragedy, adding that the first two moments "are not independent, existing as they do only for the third moment beyond the comic and the tragic: the production of something new entails a dramatic repetition which excludes even the hero" (Deleuze 1994, p. 92). He also and explicitly refers to Marx, pointing out that he has reversed the order suggested by the latter: within the whole dynamics of repetition, comedy (mechanical, stereotyped repetition) comes before tragedy (repetition as metamorphosis). To which he adds a very important remark:

> However, once the first two elements acquire an abstract independence or become genres, then the comic succeeds the tragic as though the failure of metamorphosis, raised to the absolute, presupposed an earlier metamorphosis already completed. (ibid., p. 92)

In other words, comedy as genre is not simply about failure, about the hero's ludicrous but stubborn, "mechanical" attempts to accomplish something which he is absolutely not up to. Instead, it functions in the background of something that has always-already succeeded, and draws its power from there. This remark is important not only because it points to an important fact that I hinted at in the beginning of this section—a possibility of repetition that is constitutive for the comic genre as such—but also because it indicates a way of redeeming what is otherwise rather problematic in the Deleuzian account of comic and tragic repetition. From what we have been able to say about comedy so far, it clearly follows that comedy moves broadly in the register of success, not in the register of failure and of the hero's not being up to his task. The task might indeed be much too big for the hero, and the action full of various misunderstandings, intentions that misfire, and so on, yet comedy is still essentially governed by what, in and through all these misadventures, inevitably succeeds. It does indeed presuppose a realization (an already accomplished metamorphosis), and does not consist simply of vain and endless attempts to accomplish it. Also—and this time in relation to tragedy—it is difficult to accept the claim that the tragic hero is "equal" to his act. Even if we leave aside a tragedy like *Hamlet*, entirely constructed around the hero's not being equal to his act, and focus on a more common type of tragic heroes and heroines, who are indeed determined to act and do act (sometimes even precipitately), a crucial fact remains: there is always something in their actions which absolutely surpasses and exceeds them (as subjects), that is, something to which they are never equal, something that is ultimately the very cause of their tragedy.

If we now move on to the third mode of repetition posited by Deleuze, to which he ascribes the whole meaning of the Nietzschean eternal return, we could say that it constitutes something like a concept–project, a concept-yet-to-become (what it is), a concept-yet-to-be-realized. It also involves—again on a much more elaborated conceptual level—the Marxian diagnosis of the inner relentlessness and "terror" of revolutionary repetition. We have already seen that the eternal return cannot simply mean the eternal return of the same (of some identity), but involves an additional turn: the only sameness is the constitutive difference of the return itself. Related to this is Deleuze's big invention in respect to this Nietzschean notion, the invention of the *selectiveness* of the eternal return (developed in his book on Nietzsche). Not only does the notion of the eternal return not imply that everything (that once was) eternally returns, it refers to a type of repetition which, through repetition itself, actively ejects, expels, everything that belongs to repetition as such (to the first two modes of repetition).

> The condition of the action by default does not return; the condition of the agent by metamorphoses does not return; all that returns, the eternal return, is the *unconditional* in the product. The expulsive and selective force of the eternal return, its centrifugal force, consists of distributing the repetition among the three times of the pseudo-cycle, but also of ensuring that the first two repetitions do not return. . . . The negative, the similar and the analogous are repetitions, but they do not return, forever driven away by the wheel of the eternal return. (Deleuze 1994, p. 297)

Or, as Deleuze also puts it: The wheel in the eternal return is at once both production of repetition on the basis of difference and selection of difference on the basis of repetition. Taking into account the link between repetition and difference, we could say that what is at stake here is repetition as inner differentiation (or "purge") of Difference. In a kind of political caricature, Deleuze's reading of Nietzsche on this point could be described as "Stalin versus Mao Zedong"; not "let a thousand flowers of difference bloom!", but rather: "let the inner differentiation of differences do away with all false differences, to the benefit of the only one that is real!" Indeed, Deleuze's treatment of the difference in *Difference and Repetition* is light years away from the contemporary politico-ideological glorification of differences with which his philosophy is often associated.

The tone sometimes gets even stronger. Deleuze talks about "definite elimination," and we also find this sentence: "Not only does the eternal return not make everything return, it causes those who fail the test to perish" (Deleuze 1994, p. 299). Strictly (conceptually) speaking, this last sentence does not make much sense—it does not make much sense since Deleuze holds the eternal return to be, in principle, beyond everything that could be called ego, subject, hero, man, woman, person. The world of eternal return is "the world of impersonal individualities and pre-individual singularities" (ibid., p. 299)—that is to say, a world where it makes no sense to talk about a heroic passing of the test. This points to a certain difficulty of Deleuze's position: he needs a purely impersonal, asubjective force (the "eternal return") to take on the charge of watching over the realization of a whole series of predicates, the preference of which is very much embedded in a strong subjective (and political) context and stance (horizontally rhizomatic versus vertically hierarchical; positive excess versus negativity and lack; multiplicity versus one; nomadic versus static; different versus similar or identical; exceptional versus ordinary . . .). In mentioning the subjective determination of this list, I do not wish to submit its "objective validity" to relativism, nor to accuse Deleuze of hiding a subjective agenda behind supposedly neutral forces. The hesitation is more conceptually fundamental: can these predicates be handed over to realization by a perfectly asubjective, neutral force, without losing the very edge that sustains them? The opposition to or subtraction from the regime of the laws, which so strongly dominates Deleuze's philosophical project, ultimately culminates in the realm of an *absolute* law, a law as the thing in itself, which rules through an immediate necessity. It is through this absolute necessity that the "positive" predicates listed above will be realized, and it seems that nothing can prevent this realization.

Thus the centrifugal force of repetition in its most radical form not only introduces the difference at the very core of repetition, but also "realizes" this difference—it realizes it by extracting repetition itself from repetition, by extracting what is new from the mechanism of repetition that produced it. This is what could be described, in Deleuze, as a concept–project, the latter being no less than the project of realized ontology ("However, the only realized Ontology—in other words, the univocity of being—is repetition" [Deleuze 1996, p. 303]). Difference is the only and original being, yet at the same time it (still) needs to be realized, that is to say, *repeated*, and thus separated from all the metaphysical and dialectical baggage that constitutes the history of Being and of its thought. This motive that implies an imperative to realize the Real (through repetition), the motive of the realization of ontology, is a very intriguing aspect of Deleuze's thought, which I will not discuss here. Let me just say, in a very cursory way, that on the level of realized ontology there is no place for comedy or tragedy (as modes of repetition). For they both belong to being such as it is—and being, such as it is, is a being that is fundamentally out of joint, whereas the realized (that is, the truly repeated) being is the being (= difference) that becomes absolutely one with itself.

If we now move on to Lacan, the first and obvious question might be: How is he situated in relation to the (Deleuzian) thesis about the primary, original character of difference? In a certain way this is, of course, also Lacan's thesis. Yet there is a crucial difference: for Lacan the primacy of difference is the primacy of the symbolic cut; whereas for Deleuze, and especially the Deleuze of *Difference and Repetition*, the primary and fundamental difference functions as real, even as the only Real. Perhaps a more precise way of putting it would be to say that the Deleuzian conceptual project aims precisely at abolishing the difference between the Symbolic and the Real, that it involves a kind of "realization of the Symbolic," or a becoming-real of the Symbolic (a very direct consequence of this is the prominence of psychosis in general and schizophrenia in particular in the Deleuzian universe: psychosis implies precisely that symbolic relations appear as real—like "nerves" and "cosmic rays" in the case of President Schreber). Related to this is the fact that the Deleuzian Real is very different from the Lacanian Real: whereas in Deleuze it ultimately refers to the cosmic whole as an inherently productive self-differentiating substance, which is also to say to the process of becoming, in Lacan it is neither a substance nor a process. Rather, it is something that interrupts a process, something closer to a stumbling block; it is an impossibility in the structure of the field of reality.

To say that for Lacan the symbolic cut is primary does not mean that the other two registers (the Real and the Imaginary) gradually develop from it. They all emerge at the same time, and perhaps the best way of conceiving how this might work is with the help of the following example. In *Seminar XI* Lacan refers to the dialectic of the silence and the cry, pointing out that "the cry does not stand out against a background of silence, but on the contrary makes the silence emerge as silence" (Lacan 1986, p. 26). This remark is quite well known, yet what is usually missed about it is that it does not involve simply a dialectic of two elements—instead, we are immediately dealing with three elements. Which three?

The cry here is the signifier as the carrier of the symbolic cut, and with it of all subsequent symbolic differentiations. The background which gets constituted with this cry and appears, from a later perspective, as the lost preexisting primordial Unity is the Imaginary. The effect of the symbolic cut itself—that is to say, the consistency of the cut as such—is the Real. The split, the gap that the Symbolic leaves in what it constitutes when it gets constituted itself, is the (only) Real. The Real is the impasse, the split at the very heart of the symbolic structure. This also implies that not all differences are symbolic, although they all depend on the emergence of the symbolic cut. Let us illustrate this with the following schema. The three Lacanian registers of the Symbolic, the Imaginary, and the Real could also be said to correspond to three different kinds of repetition. Schematically: the Imaginary is the register of repetition as similarity, resemblance; the Symbolic is the register of repetition as identity (which has nothing to do with resem-

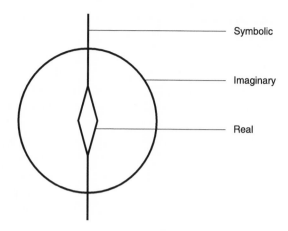

blance, but depends on a singular mark or trait); the Real is the register of repetition as coincidence, rupture, surprise (one could also say: of sameness as novelty). In psychoanalytic practice the imaginary register does not play an essential role, whereas the Symbolic and the Real are very heavily involved.

Lacan works out the distinction between the mode of repetition involved in these two registers with the help of his specific reading of the Aristotelian distinction between *tyche* and *automaton*. *Automaton* belongs to the symbolic register and refers to the automatic side of repetition, to the iterability of signs, as well as to the insistence on the repetition of satisfaction characteristic of the pleasure principle. *Tyche*, on the other hand, rather implies contingency, accident, coincidence—that is, repetition as involved in the drive (existing beyond the pleasure principle), and originating in a contingent encounter with the Real.[10] This Lacanian elaboration is often read as opposing the two terms, accentuating the "good" *tyche* against the "bad" *automaton*. However, Mladen Dolar has suggested a much more interesting and conceptually convincing way of envisaging the relationship between the two repetitions, a way that corresponds very closely to the relationship between the Symbolic and the Real as sketched above via the example of the cry.

> Yet the whole point is, I think, that one shouldn't read it as two different sorts of repetition or as placed on two different levels; they only exist together and intertwined. To put it simply, *tyche* is the gap of the *automaton*. In the tiny gap between one occurrence and the next one, a bit of real is produced. In every repetition there is already, in a minimal way, the emergence of that which escapes symbolization, the haphazard contingent object appears which spoils the mere repeating of the same, so the same which returns is never the same although we couldn't tell it apart from its previous occurrence by any of the positive features or distinguishing marks. There is a contingent bit which dwells in the gap, which is produced by the very gap, and this imperceptible bit is the stuff that comedy puts to maximum use. (Dolar 2005a, p. 200)

To say that *tyche* is the gap in *automaton* is indeed a thesis that is very well supported by the existence of comedy, which thrives on exposing the heterogeneity produced by automatic repetition as well as—once it has brought it to light—on ignoring it in a very comically noticeable way. But before we pick up the thread of comedy again, let us take a step backwards to the question of why it is that repetition is so relevant to psychoanalysis to begin with.

I have already said that repetition has a specific significance vis-à-vis representation. Indeed, Freud very soon discovered an important limit of representation (as the work of remembering and interpretation in analysis). Some symptoms persist, and keep repeating beyond conscious representation of the trauma involved in them. Unconscious formations can be successfully deciphered, and their causes explained, but the problem nevertheless persists, sometimes in a modified form, transposed in new articulations. One of the Freudian answers to this was the hypothesis of a primary repression, *Urverdrängung*, a kind of singular subjective condition and directing principle of all subsequent, proper repressions. In what way? Primary repression involves the notorious *Vorstellungsrepräsentanz*, "representative of the representation" of the drive that has never been conscious, and induces a fixation; the representative in question persists unaltered from then onwards. Now, the second stage of repression or "*repression proper* affects mental derivatives of the repressed representative, or such trains of thought as, originating elsewhere, have come into associative connection with it" (Freud 2001, p. 148). In other words, what is primarily repressed is not the drive itself, or the affect, or its representation, but the subject's marker of this representation. The critical point about this is not to confound this marker with something that the subject saw or experienced in reality, and repressed because of its intimate connection with the affect in its traumatic pressure. The "primarily repressed" marker or representative of the drive is something that has never been conscious, and has never been part of any subjective experience, but constitutes its ground. The logic of repression by association is the logic of what Freud calls repression proper, whereas primary repression is precisely not a repression in this sense. In it the causality usually associated with the unconscious is turned upside-down: it is not that we repress a signifier because of a traumatic experience related to it, rather, it is because this signifier is repressed that we can experience something as traumatic (not simply as painful, frustrating, and so on), and repress it. In other words, at some fundamental level the cause of repression is repression. One must congratulate Freud for this speculative tour de force with which he avoided the traps on the slippery ground of the question of origins (of the unconscious), the traps of its full linear deduction. There is of course a strong causal chain that leads from somatic functions and dysfunctions—combined with some other factors—to the unconscious proper. Freud never retracted from this kind of analysis—on the contrary. Yet he also recognized a certain constitutive circularity involved in the constitution of the subject—a circularity that points to an irreducible leap in this constitution. The hypothesis of a primary repression is not meant to invite us—once we have brought to light all sorts of different "ordinary" repressions—to dig even deeper in search of their ultimate Cause or Ground, but instead to ground the unconscious in the very leap of (its) causality.

Lacan took up the notion of primary repression on his own theoretical ground, and linked it to his conception of alienation as constitutive of subjectivity. Alienation is not the cause of primary repression; rather, it is its effect or result. To put it simply: the subjective split between the signifying dyad constitutive of alienation is the result of the fall of the first signifier, which is to say of the signifier as *one*. The logic of the signifier (and the subject as what one signifier represents for another signifier) starts only with two, it starts with the signifying dyad. On the level of the first signifier there is as yet no subject and not signifying logic or chain. The latter, however, does not occur by means of a second signifier being added to the first; it emerges by means of the "repression" of the first signifier, and emerges *at its place*. More precisely, what emerges at the place of the repressed signifier-one is the signifying dyad through which the subject is constituted, and stuck in its fundamental either–or. Yet alienation does not imply only an "either–or," a necessary choice, it involves a forced choice, exemplified by Lacan in the saying "Your money or your life!"—one can only choose one term or lose both. And this is the level on which primary repression (or, rather, its effects) operates: as that on account of which the choice is never neutral but originally biased, excluding one set (that of the meaningless being of the drives) and instituting the other (that of meaning). The forced choice of meaning is also a way out of the mortifying and alienating grip of the signifying dyad, because it already involves a set or a chain of signifiers and, with it, a circular sliding of the subject. In schematic terms, we are thus dealing with three steps or three levels involved in the constitution of the subject: the prememorial or presubjective primarily repressed signifier-one; the signifying dyad that emerges at its place and gives form to alienation constitutive of subjectivity; and the signifying chain already implied in one of the two terms of the signifying dyad, but activated only with the forced choice of this term. This is why, when the subject comes to exist, she exists only in the Other, through the signifying chain, which is to say as metonymic meaning(s) of the originally missing signifier. This is the level of interpretation (in analysis, as well as in general): since the subject emerges are pure difference in relation to her own being, she then strives to appropriate the latter by way of meaning constituted in the Other, and of its endless metonymy. Interpretation leads us to and through different forms/meanings developed around the subject's singular lack of being.

Repetition is situated on a different level from this metonymic sliding: it is essentially the repetition of the signifying dyad—that is to say, repetition of fundamental alienation, as well as of its other side and condition, namely primary repression. So the point is not that the constitutively missing (primarily repressed) signifier is the cause of repetition. Repetition is not the result of a failed representation, or the result of (primary) repression. It is not that the lack of the "right" signifier induces repetition (which would stop if the right signifier were found again). Rather, repetition and primary repression are part of one and the same process.

If primary repression is the repression of a "representative" or of a signifier (as pure mark), what does this imply for the relationship between representation and repetition? Here the psychoanalytic perspective differs from the Deleuzian: true, repetition is beyond representation proper, it is completely different from and irreducible to it—yet it is also inseparable from it, for it constitutes its other side. Repetition is always a repetition of representation (the signifying dyad), but it is also a repetition of the inherent gap or interval between its terms, which is the very locus of surprise in repetition, of the Real encountered in it. In other words, here we come back to the relationship between *tyche* and *automaton* as sketched out above: *tyche* is the gap of *automaton*; despite their radical heterogeneity, the two cannot be simply separated. There is a contingent object that dwells in the gap of *automaton* as repetition of the signifying dyad.

But what is it that repetition repeats? If it essentially repeats the signifying dyad of alienation, this implies that it repeats a certain configuration. But by repeating this configuration it also repeats the Real of its other side, that is to say, the subject's unrepresented presence in the Real.

In order to illustrate and explain this further, let us look at two examples of repetition quoted by Lacan. The first example is the famous child's game discussed by Freud, known as fort–da. The child (who happens to be Freud's grandson) plays with a small cotton reel, linked to him by a thread which he holds, and with the help of which he alternately throws the reel away and pulls it back to him while mumbling something that sounds like fort–da ("away–here" or "there–here"). Lacan refuses the simple reading according to which the bobbin represents the child's mother, so that the whole game would be designed for the child to get some mastery over her presence and (traumatic) absence. The repetition at stake does not symbolize a need that might demand the return of the mother. If the mother's departure is traumatic for the child, it is not simply because of her absence, but because of the split (Spaltung) it causes in the subject himself. And it is this split that the child's game repeats—he replays, repeats, the fundamental alienation. In this game of fort–da both terms are essential, for it is with both that the child designates the gap, the jumping of which he plays at. He plays at jumping this gap by repeatedly "sending over" something that functions as a detachable part of himself, which is a precise definition of the object a.

> If the young subject can practice this game of fort–da, it is precisely be-cause he does not practice it at all, for no subject can grasp this radi-cal articulation. He practices it with the help of a small bobbin, that it to say, with the object a. The function of the exercise with this object refers to an alienation, and not to some supposed mastery, which is difficult to imagine being increased in an endless repetition, whereas the endless repetition that is in question reveals the radical vacillation of the subject. (Lacan 1986, p. 239)

Several important points come to light in the perspective of this example. First, it makes it easier to see that repetition is—as sug-gested above—essentially the repetition of a certain configura-tion, not simply or directly the repetition of some element(s). It is the game itself that is the Repräsentanz of the Vorstellung.[11] We could also say that repetition exists because there is no linear genesis of the subject (or, to put it the other way around: because there is a subject—the latter being precisely the effect of a dysfunction in the purely linear causality). The genesis of a subject always and necessarily involves a leap, and repetition at its fundamental is repetitious jumping, going back and forth between the edges of this leap. On this particular level repetition is clearly opposed to fantasy, which consists in filling in the gap in question, and transforming the constitutive leap into a linear story. Also, at its most fundamental, fantasy is fantasy about the origins (of the subject).

In relation to this questions I am tempted to make a brief digression, and to suggest that the play scene in *Hamlet* (the mousetrap, the play-within-the-play) is not simply a representation but also, and more importantly, repetition at its purest. This is well illustrated by the fact that the play scene itself is structured as repetition—not only does it repeat another play (*The Murder of Gonzago*), but the latter is performed twice: first silently, as dumb show, and again with words and more acting. The dumb-show version as it appears in the play is, in the extreme economy of its means and its extent, a very clear pointer to the underlying logic of the repetition:

> Enter a KING and a QUEEN very lovingly; the QUEEN embracing him, and he her. She kneels, and makes show of protestation unto him. He takes her up, and declines his head upon her neck; lays him down upon a bank of flowers: she, seeing him asleep, leaves him. Anon comes in a fellow, takes off his crown, kisses it, and pours poison in the KING'S ears, and exit. The QUEEN returns; finds the KING dead, and makes passionate action. The POISONER, with some two or three MUTES, comes in again, seemingly to lament with her. The dead body is carried away. The POISONER woos the QUEEN with gifts: she seems loth and unwilling awhile, but in the end accepts his love.

There is something in this piece of text that sounds—not exactly dreamlike, but very much like an account of a dream that one might make in analysis, like many reported by Freud in his work. It is, at the same time, extremely lapidary and abstract, yet it also contains some curious details (like the king lying down "upon a bank of flowers"—a reference, one might say, not only to the "orchard" mentioned by the ghost of Hamlet's father, but also to his being "cut off in the blossom of his sin"). The account is full of missing links that we fill in with our knowledge of the story, but which become rather striking if we make an effort to take and read the account such as it is, without its well-known background. There is also an almost comic quality in the reductionism of this account, in the mechanical speed with which the peaks of this monumental story appear before us.

If we draw this comparison a little further, we might say that, like the work of analysis, Shakespeare's play equips us with a way of relating the "manifest" form of this story to its "latent" thoughts and to (supposedly) real events behind it. Yet—also as in analysis—this is far from exhausting what is at stake. There is also, and not surprisingly, a playlike element of repetition involved, which accounts for much of the scene's captivating character. If we stop to think about it, it is abundantly clear that the fascination of this scene is not exhausted by the play representing, drawing up a sketch of what really (but secretly) happened. Indeed, in relation to the play scene the narrative focus is so much on the murderous king, and on the attempt to catch his conscience in the "mousetrap" of the play, that we tend to lose sight of the role that this peculiar performance, in its very repetition, plays for Hamlet. By staging, even directing, the play, and getting an appropriate response from Claudius, Hamlet gets more than just a (firm?) confirmation of the words of his father's ghost. He gets to play at his own game of fort–da, for this is precisely what the play scene is for Hamlet. The object which vacillates, appears, and disappears in the folds of this family drama is Hamlet himself. As is otherwise blatantly clear from the play as a whole, its events stir up the question of Hamlet's being: To be or not to be is not simply a reflection on the possibility of suicide (as an action yet to be accomplished), it is also an articulation of another kind of vacillation between being and nonbeing: a vacillation in which the subject's nonbeing is already there, as part of his very existence. To be—not to be, here I am, and there I am not. . . .

There is also another point to be made concerning the relationship between theater and repetition. For it seems that there is an inherently theatrical element involved in repetition—theatrical in the sense of belonging to theater, not in the sense of being melodramatic, exaggerated, or affected. This might be explained, at least to some extent, by the point made above: that repetition is essentially repetition of a configuration; that it doesn't represent anything, but is itself the very content of what it represents: repetition itself is the *Repräsentanz* of the *Vorstellung*. This relationship between repetition and representation, in which repetition precedes the represented, is very well expressed in French theater terminology. In theater, we start with "repetitions," for rehearsals are called *repetitions*, and we end up with *la première*, with the first (performance or the first night). Repetitions do not repeat some first occurrence but, rather, lead up to it. . . .

Let us now return to Lacan and to the second example of repetition, which refers to a strange habit that many small children share: they demand not only to be told the same story again and again, but also that it should be *textually* the same, with a distinct consistency in the details of its telling. It is not enough that it is repeated in its meaning and its plot, it has to be repeated literally. In relation to this, Lacan also immediately makes the essential point:

> Whatever, in repetition, is varied, modulated, merely alienates us from its meaning. The adult, and even the more advanced child, demands something new in his activities, in his games. But this sliding-away (*glissement*) conceals what is the true secret of the ludic, namely, the most radical diversity constituted by repetition in itself. (Lacan 1986, p. 61)

What exactly is at stake in this difference between repetition through variety and textual repetition? The briefest answer would be: the difference between the fact that we *can* tell something in hundred different ways, and the fact that we *cannot*, absolutely not (not even by literally repeating it) tell something in only one way. And this is how the signifying dyad of alienation is repeated in this case. Textual, mechanical, stereotyped repetition is the mode in which the young subject, behind the scenes of the seemingly monotonous story, repeats the exciting story of a fundamental split or incongruity in her own being and meaning. On this level, Lacan's point seems to converge with Deleuze's principal thesis from *Difference and Repetition*: the persistent failure of repetition ultimately brings us to the conclusion that the only thing that repeats without fail is difference itself. Lacan and Deleuze differ, however, on one crucial point which concerns precisely the question of failure in repetition. For Deleuze, the apparent failure or impossibility of repetition leads, in a switch of perspective, to the posting of the difference as pure affirmation: the only thing that is repeated is difference, the only sameness is the sameness of difference itself. The seeming failure of repetition is in fact the triumph of difference, which is then posited, in Deleuzian ontology, as the very being of repetition. The motor of repetition is not some kind of negativity (we do not repeat because we fail), but the affirmation of difference itself. The Lacanian conception takes a different, arguably more radical turn. Lacan's point is also not—and here he agrees with Deleuze—that failure is the motor of repetition (that we repeat because we missed the first time), but neither it is that difference is the being that repeats itself and wants repetition. There is something else involved. If we simplify things and relate them to the example above, we could say: the child demands repetition because its failure nevertheless realizes something, and this something is precisely what he wanted to see, appearing in the form in which he wanted, or was able, to see it. In other words: the failure of repetition itself fails at some point, or, *something disturbs the pure failure of repetition*: something fleeting, elusive, something perceptible at one moment and gone the next. And this something is what the subject wants to see, again and again and again. It fascinates her; she never tires of it. This something is related to *tyche*, and it is also what Lacan calls the object *a* in its dimension of the Real, that is to say, as the subject's own shooting star in the Real, the object via which, for a moment, the subject sees herself on the outside. And it is precisely this object that constitutes the "radical diversity" that Lacan emphasizes in the above quote, linking it to repetition. It is a diversity that belongs to a different order than variety and novelty.

RETURN TO COMEDY

If we now return to the question of comedy, I would propose the following thesis: if the variation of the story, the colorfulness, the variety of the game, the demand for something new (that we experience as older children and adults)—if all these somehow obscure the radical diversity/heterogeneity implied in the demand for textual repetition, then comedy is precisely a return to this kind of repetition. It is, among other things, a repetition of this repetition. This feature also helps to explain, at least in part, why comedy has often been seen as something of a rather "lower" order, as "childish" and "stupid."

Before we now embark on a discussion of the difference between tragedy and comedy from the point of view of repetition, one preliminary remark is necessary. Tragedy is not—at least since Shakespeare, and particularly (although not exclusively) with Shakespeare—a monolithic genre. In tragedies we can find perfectly comic sequences (passages, episodes) which do not transform tragedy into comedy (or into tragicomedy), but exist in their specificity without affecting the structure of the tragic genre. To take the example of *Hamlet* again, there is the whole first part of the graveyard scene, with the two clowns discussing Ophelia's death. Their dialogue—despite its somber topic—is a perfect example of comic dialogue, starting from the point that Ophelia, given that she would have a Christian burial, must have "drown'd herself in her own defense," passing through a discussion of how this might be accomplished, and culminating in denouncing the privileged class for their having "countenance in this world to drown or hang themselves, more than their even Christian." Also, most of Hamlet's interactions with Polonius are of a comic nature. Take this famous (and short) one, which immediately precedes the play scene:[12]

HAMLET: My lord, you play'd once i'th'university, you say?

POLONIUS: That did I, my lord; and was accounted a good actor.

HAMLET: And what did you enact?

POLONIUS: I did enact Julius Caesar: I was kill'd i'th'Capitol; Brutus kill'd me.

HAMLET: It was a brute part of him to kill so capital a calf there.—Be the players ready?

This brief exchange is perfectly comical, in the sense that it is self-standing and does not need the background of the rest of the tragedy to strike us as comical. The important point to make for our present discussion is simply that such comic sequences are in principle clearly separable from the tragic structure, and could be considered within a discussion of comedy. They might be essential for examining this or that (tragic) play in its integrity, but are not essential for examining its tragic structure. For they come, in the composition of the play, from a distinctly different source (and are not developed "out of tragedy," so to speak, and on its ground). As for comedy, it can of course include, if not exactly tragic episodes, at least episodes that are perfectly serious, or lyrical, or something else. When we talk about differences between "tragedy" and "comedy," we are thus referring to the structure that supports this or that genre in a play, and "justifies" this classification, not to the sum of all the episodes involved in this or that play.

To return to repetition: it is a commonplace to say that comedy is full of "mechanical," textual repetitions, whereas we do not really find this kind of repetition in tragedy. But perhaps we can find something more interesting and conceptually productive if we formulate this slightly differently: tragedy cannot stand textual, mechanical repetition, whereas comedy not only stands it, but thrives on it. A tragedy that repeats itself is no longer tragedy (and even if its repetition is absolutely horrible, the latter is deprived of its epic dignity, essential to tragedy proper). Yet if tragedy that repeats itself is no longer tragedy, this does not make it comedy. This point is very important: comedy is not a repetition of tragedy, it is a repetition of something structurally prior to or independent of tragedy. There is no direct passage from tragedy to comedy; we do not get comedy by repeating tragedy. In this respect, we must be careful to distinguish between comic sequences within tragedy (as described above) and what is usually called tragicomedy. The repetition of tragedy falls into this latter category of tragicomedy.

The genre of tragicomedy, which has experienced such a significant rise all through modernity (and postmodernity), is to be understood in the perspective of the repetition of tragedy (not in the perspective of the development of comedy). It is a development that takes place within the tragic paradigm. It involves the recognition of the fact that the tragic itself (with all its epic splendor) is ultimately but a mask of the really miserable, a mask that cannot survive its own repetition. The repetition of tragic events deprives the latter of their aura and transforms them into something common, unexceptional. The really miserable is not even tragic, and does not possess tragic grandeur. This "worse than tragedy" is one of the great experiences/discoveries of modernity: a bare life deprived of its singular Master-Signifier which could inscribe death in the dimension of, for example, honor and dignity, and put it in relationship to a "second death." A thing can be a terrible and devastating in its repetition (the repetition does not necessarily take that away), but it is no longer tragic, and this, we could say, constitutes a supreme tragedy of modernity. Paul Claudel, for example, explored the ontological dimension of this end of tragedy, whereas tragicomedy explores its mechanical dimension, repeating tragedy beyond tragedy, which reminds us of comedy. Yet again, I strongly believe that we should resist the temptation to conclude from there that this kind of repetition leads, from itself, to comedy. Although it might indeed make us laugh, it is not comedy. It is possible only against the background of tragedy. What defines it perfectly is the term "tragedy's comedy."[13] Tragedy's comedy very much exists, and has also drawn some serious critical attention. Yet I would maintain that it is essentially a subgenre, or even a successor, of tragedy. On the other hand, what this book aims at circumscribing and discussing in its own right is something else: namely "comedy's comedy."

The question of repetition debated in this chapter can help us to define some of the crucial elements of the difference between tragedy and comedy. We could say that there is a common sensitive point around which both revolve, or to which both give form: the real impasse of the symbolic structure, the constitutive leap of subjectivity, the schism of being and meaning as the other side of primary repression. Tragedy is essentially the work of sublimation, in the precise sense of elevating a singular subjective destiny to that place of the symbolic structure that constitutes its blind spot, its inherent impasse. This is not exactly to say that tragedy "represents" this impasse with this or that exemplary story. Rather—and to borrow the Deleuzian terminology—it repeats it in disguise. This disguise is not a deformation or a mask of the real impasse: rather, the Real exists only from one mask to another. It is from this real impasse, the place of which it occupies, that the tragic mask draws its tragic splendor. Now, if we apply here, in a second step, a mechanical, textual repetition, we will repeat only the disguise, not the place it occupies. In other words, repetition will fail to repeat the singularity of what it is repeating, it will repeat only the empty gestures.

We could say that tragedy repeats (or reactualizes) the real impasse by giving it this or that form. In other words, tragedy repeats the universal impasse by producing (different) concrete cases of this impasse. I have already argued, in Part I above, that the concreteness of comedy lies elsewhere, whereas on this level comedy is perfectly stereotypical, it puts aside all subtleties of a situation or character, ignoring their psychological depths and motives, reducing them all to a few "unary traits," which it then plays with and repeats indefinitely. As Walter Benjamin pointed out in "Fate and Character": in a comedy like *The Miser*, for instance, we learn nothing about miserliness, the play does not make this phenomenon any more comprehensible; rather, it depicts it with an intensifying crassness, producing it in the form of a singular trait. This insightful remark is not true only in the case of comic characters, but also holds true for comic situations.

Thus, instead of deploying a subjective meaning and destiny in its constitutive disjunction with the subject's Master-Signifier (as tragedy does), comedy serves as a bunch of Master-Signifiers. Yet, in a departure from the structure of (most) jokes, Master-Signifiers enter the scene of comedy not in order to have the last word, but in order to be repeated there (as well as subjected to other comic techniques). Their repetition is not simply their affirmation. An identical reaction (of a character) repeated ten times necessarily has its repercussions on the stability of the Master-Signifier involved. And the repercussions of this kind of comic repetition usually point not in the direction of stabilizing the repeated position but, rather, in the direction of shaking it.

The first crucial step in the art of comedy is thus to create/ extract and put forward the right Master-Signifiers. That is to say, Master-Signifiers that, in all their arbitrariness, convey not simply the "essence" of a character or situation but, rather, their acute or sensitive point: the point where—like a chemical element—a character or situation remains "reactive" and/or "explosive," and is connected to other elements by a link that is never simply given, but is constantly (re)negotiated. The second crucial step in the art of comedy is the (usually antagonistic) play it constructs between these Master-Signifiers: combinations, redoublings, symmetrical and asymmetrical repetitions, irresistibly returning obstructions. . . .

In this sense, comedy is always a comedy of Master-Signifiers or, one could also say: an experimental chemistry of Master-Signifiers. This is related to another important feature of comedy: its preeminent involvement with the present. This feature has already been pointed out by Agnes Heller (Heller 2005). Comic experience is strictly bound up with the present; unlike mourning, which is deeply involved in the past and plays an important role in tragedy, there is no such central and past-oriented emotion that can be called constitutive of comic experience. This attachment to the present is also discernible in the fact that improvisation on the stage is the prerogative of comic actors ("there is no *tragedia dell'arte*, only *comedia dell'arte*," ibid., p. 13). To this I would add that comedy's link with the ever-present time is not situated only on the level of comic experience, but also on the level of structure. There are, strictly speaking, no past causes and future effects for comedy. Comedy practically never tries to explain *why* something happened, but it is extremely adept at showing *how* something functions—that is to say, it is adept at showing the mechanisms, *in the present*, that allow its functioning and perpetuation. Comic elements always react (to others) in the present, and although they usually give the impression that they *necessarily* and unavoidably react as they do, they also—since this always happens right before our eyes—display a radical contingency involved in this very necessity.

This disinterest in *why* is in fact a very intriguing feature of the structure of comedy, which replaces the cause–effect relationship and its temporal logic (before–after) with a juxtaposition of different elements, and their (active or not) connections. From this perspective, comic repetition—which is always a repetition in the present—reactivates the very ground or presupposition of a given structure, and makes it appear as an object. The latter is precisely the heterogeneous element/object produced by textual repetition (made easier by the reduction of the situation or the character to a few Master-Signifiers). Seen in this light, the difference between comedy and tragedy would be that the former repeats this singular object, whereas tragedy incorporates it into a subjective destiny. In tragedy, it appears as the *je ne sais quoi*, the mysterious singularity that endows a particular (tragic) destiny with a sublime radiance, whereas in comedy it appears as an "essential byproduct" of a character or situation. One could also say that unlike tragic *heroes*, who seem to carry this singular object within themselves, comic *characters* carry it outside themselves, so that it (more or less independently of their will and actions) hangs onto them.

To sum up: through enacting certain configurations, tragedy confronts us with the Real; it always gives the Real this or that face, the face of this or that tragic split that resonates with something in our own imagination: we experience it through the play, we can feel it. Comedy, on the other hand, does not confront us with the Real, it repeats it. It repeats it, so to speak, on the outside. And it is itself constituted as a repetition of that repetition which, in the life of a subject, precedes repetition through difference and variety, which gives color to the subject's life drama. It is a "mechanical" repetition of the subject's constitution, not its representation through an unfolding of the destiny that follows from it, a destiny which can only be repetition in disguise. It is not a representation of a subjective destiny but a repetition of the occurrence that makes the subject emerge under the sign of representation.

If we return to the psychoanalytic outlines sketched above, we could say that tragedy is essentially bound up with the different forms and meanings that a subject's destiny may take, starting from the pivotal but inaccessible point of primary repression. In psychoanalysis, this is the level of interpretation, of working through different layers and forms of one's subjective meaning and desire. But there is also the question of primary repression which constitutes the other, the reverse side of this question of interpretation and deployment of different meanings. According to Lacan, access to it is possible only as it reconstruction through repetition, through the work of repetition. The primarily repressed signifier is not something we could ever "remember," since it disappeared before (or with) the very constitution of subjective memory. It would also be wrong to say that the reconstruction of this signifier is traumatic for the subject. On the contrary, we could say that in analysis it is almost everything else (but this) that is traumatic. Here, the subject doesn't feel anything, while she can feel a lot when she is working with repressed representations, as well as when she is dealing with the compulsion to repeat, which is not in the least funny for her. The compulsion to repeat is a specific category of repetition which I shall not discuss here, except for the following brief remark. In relation to the question of comedy, compulsive repetition could be set side by side with the compulsive joking, joke-telling, jesting which is itself a rather specific, "pathological" mode of comedy. The simplest way to define this mode would be to say that in it, repetition itself is used as the veil that screens off the heterogeneous, surprising element produced by it; repetition is used as the veil that hides the real effects of the (previous) repetition. If we formulate things in this way, it becomes clearer why this kind of repetition demands its constant intensification: the more repetition there is, the more is needed to cover up what it produces as its by-product—and more, and more, and more. . . .

The fact that the reconstruction of the missing signifier is not in itself traumatic does not prevent the subject's relationship to this lack from being very much so. The point is simply that what is traumatic is not the meaning or the content of this signifier. The latter was not repressed because of its content, but in the contingency of the subject emerging in its place. The destiny of the subject is to unfold, through time, as all possible meanings of this signifier, all its masks, to be the life of all these meanings and also, perhaps, to work through them in analysis. But the crucial point is that the subject is not the sum of all these meanings, or simply their inner differentiation *qua* pure difference, and that her being is dislocated in relation to her meaning. Comic repetition is, essentially, repetition of the vacillation between these two terms of being and meaning, between "I am where I make no sense" and "I make sense where I am not." How? Comedy moves, of course, very close to a fundamental kernel of nonsense, yet the way it goes about it takes a very intriguing form: it does not try to show us the nonsense as such, which, indeed, would be a rather impossible thing to do, since this path leads only as far as revealing an absence of sense, and nonsense is something other than a mere absence of sense. Comedy knows very well, and puts into practice, the following crucial point: we really encounter nonsense only when and where *a sense surprises us.* What comedy repeats (repeats, not reveals, since revelation is not the business of comedy) in a thousand more or less ingenious ways is the very operation in which sense is produced in a genuinely erratic manner. Things make sense in a very erratic manner. Or, to put it even more directly: sense itself is an error, a product of error; sense has the structure of an error. Although the comic mechanism of repetition of this fact is more obvious in verbal comedy, it is by no means absent from other kinds.

This is also what Lacan emphasizes both in relation to jokes and in relation to repetition: not the question of novelty, but the element of surprise at some unexpected finding. Surprise is something other than novelty. We can be surprised at something that we know very well, even expect (yet when it happens [again], it surprises us)—this is one of the main comic mechanisms. What, exactly, is surprise? What is at stake in it? We could describe it precisely as a moment of disorientation, a momentary suspension in which the subject vacillates between his being and his meaning. It is a moment at which it is no longer clear on which side we are standing—are we the audience of a joke, or something in it? Are we spectators of a picture, or some spot on it? . . . Yet again: this disorientation is the effect of some sense emerging in an unexpected place and not, for instance, the effect of an utter loss of sense.

When a child demands that his parents should textually repeat the story of the previous evening, he expects—as strange as it might sound—a surprise. And he gets it.

Comedy is a practice that repeats and satisfies this demand—in the "laboratory conditions" of its genre, but not outside any relation to the Real. Comic findings and their endless repetition, the repetition of their surprise—all these constitute a practice which does not stage the difficulty, the impediment, of the subject's relation to the Real, but repeats it. It repeats, endlessly repeats the schism of subject and object *a* (qua her being)—not so that the subject recognizes herself in this object (there is precisely nothing to "recognize" here); not in order to force a psychotic falling of the subject into the object; but repeating it at the very limit of their incongruence.

It is only when things become very serious, and we come as close as possible to the Real of this schism between the subject and her being, that comedy and true comic repetition appear. Precisely because we are dealing with an articulation that concerns the subject in her very constitution, this articulation is not accessible in any way but through (comic) repetition. The path to it does not lead through flames and hell, through burning of the flesh, or through the Passion of Christ, but through something much less deeply felt, albeit absolutely fundamental.

We are often told that comedy is possible only when the things we see on the stage do not truly concern us, and that the condition of comedy is our indifference and uninvolvement. As a conclusion to these reflections on repetition, I would suggest a different perspective: things that really concern us, things that concern the very kernel of our being, can be watched and performed only as comedy, as an impersonal play with the object. The impersonal in comedy is the *subject itself*. And the indifference is not the pathos-driven distancing at the very point when we are most affected/hurt, but is, rather, akin to that unaffectedness which is at stake in primary repression, insofar as primary repression is not the subject's repression, but coincides with and determines the constitution of the subject. In other words, if the dead serious can be approached only in comedy, this is not because any other approach would be too terrifying and would crush us completely, destroy us, but because it would miss the crucial point. For what is at stake—that is to say, what this repetition repeats—is not a reduction of ourselves (and of all that we are) to a nonbeing, not the destruction of our being, but its *emergence*—its emergence outside meaning, yet inextricably from it.

(Essential) Appendix: The Phallus

[Tragedy] certainly began in improvisations—as did
also Comedy; the one originating with the authors of
the Dithyramb, the other with those of the phallic songs,
which still survive as institutions in many of our cities.
—Aristotle, *Poetics*

The *depth* which Spirit brings forth from within . . . and
the ignorance of this consciousness about what it really
is saying, are the same conjunction of the high and the
low which, in the living being, Nature naively expresses
when it combines the organ of its highest fulfilment, the
organ of generation, with the organ of urination.
—Hegel, *Phenomenology of Spirit*

ENJOYMENT *EX MACHINA*

In our discussion so far we have linked comedy with the following configuration: there is a cut, a break of some imaginary Unity or One, followed by the play with the two that come to light in this break. The nature of this play is such that it makes two points at the same time: it shows that the two in question are inherently linked and cannot be completely separated, but also that, hard as they might try, the two can never fuse ("back") into an unproblematic One. In short, when in comedy some (imaginary) Oneness or Unity splits in two, the sum of these two parts never again amounts to the inaugural One; there is a surplus that emerges in this split, and constantly disturbs the One. We could say that the singular mathematics of comedy is based upon the following axiom:

$$\frac{1}{2} + \frac{1}{2} = 1 + x \quad \text{(where x designates what I call the comic object).}$$

From there we can deduce no less than the Formula of the comic object:

$$x = 1 - \left(\frac{1}{2} + \frac{1}{2} \right),$$

and add (I hope mathematicians will forgive me this speculative addition) that as long as $x = 0$, there is no comic object and no comedy. Comedy implies the situation in which x is bigger (or smaller) than 0.

As far as comedy is concerned, we can regret the fact that in the history of philosophy a founding text on comedy is lacking (or we can—as Umberto Eco did—make an epic story out of it, promoting the lost second book of Aristotle's *Poetics* to the most famous nonexistent book). Still, if we leave aside the possibility that the loss of the founding Text on comedy is the very *gag* that founds and inaugurates comedy itself, there is yet another possibility: that we are not looking in the right place. If we recognize the basic matrix of comedy in the difficulties involved in producing a One out of the sum of two halves, and in the unexpected third element that comes between them, we can hardly fail to remember that there is one great and fundamental philosophical text which, in one of its parts, deals precisely with these questions. And if, moreover, we bear in mind that the *porte-parole* of the part in question is none other than Aristophanes, the greatest Greek comedy writer, it seems that we are on the right track. The text that I have in mind is, of course, Plato's *Symposium*.

It is a well-known fact that the topic of Plato's *Symposium* is love, and I have no intention of performing some spectacular reinterpretation, revealing that its real topic is actually comedy. There is also no doubt that in the dramaturgy of this dialogue it is Socrates' speech that both constitutes its climax and presents Plato's views on the subject. But the fact remains that there are many others besides Socrates who speak, and that while they talk about love, they also talk about themselves and about what has influenced their views (the doctor's speech, for example, is heavily influenced by the fact that it is a doctor who is speaking . . .). And there is another, even more curious fact: despite the brilliance and the philosophical (as well as psychoanalytic) significance and weight of Socrates' speech, it was Aristophanes' speech (in all its mythological, fantasmatic, or buffoonish dimensions) that stole the show and became the most famous part of the *Symposium*, the only part that everybody knows and that is often (mistakenly) presented as Plato's view on love. (I am, of course, referring to the famous story about love as searching for our other, lost half.)

The comedian's—Aristophanes'—performance at this (first?) philosophical symposium is definitely a show, an act in itself,[1] which deserved all the attention it got, although this attention, rather unfortunately, tended to miss a crucial point of this performance: the precise point that links Aristophanes' speech on love with comedy.

The usual précis of the speech is familiar enough: In the beginning, human beings were a rounded Oneness composed or fused together from two halves; they were "whole," self-satisfied and self-sufficient beings, and this led them to arrogance and insolence, of which the gods disapproved. So they decided to split human beings in half. Since that time, each half longs for its other half. Love, which emerges when we find our other half, is simply this longing once again to become One with our other half. In this version of the story, the other we encounter in love is thus a complement supposed to make good the subjective lack.

In *The Four Fundamental Concepts of Psycho-Analysis*, Lacan—rather surprisingly—accepts this cursory version of Aristophanes' speech, and accords it no more than this critical remark:

> Aristophanes' myth pictures the pursuit of the complement for us in a moving, and misleading way, by articulating that it is the other, one's sexual other half, that the living being seeks in love. To this mythical representation of the mystery of love, analytic experience substitutes the search by the subject, not of the sexual complement, but of the part of himself, lost forever, that is constituted by the fact that he is only a sexed living being, and that he is no longer immortal. (Lacan 1986, p. 205)

There is nothing surprising about the point Lacan is making here: (human) sexuality, far from following the logic of complementarity and symmetry, breaks with it at the very outset, and quite fundamentally. "There is no sexual relationship," as Lacan puts it in his well-known dictum; there is no stable formula regulating (and guaranteeing) the relationship between sexual "partners." This is why, in another famous dictum, love necessarily involves "giving that which one doesn't have."

What is surprising about the quote from Lacan is that it reduces Aristophanes' speech to the complementarity thesis, leaving aside a very significant detail which Lacan himself had carefully pointed out three years earlier (in his commentary on the *Symposium* in the *Transference* seminar). In order to appreciate this detail, let us take a closer look at Aristophanes' story.

Cutting human beings into two (an action for which the gods had very concrete economic and security reasons: "I shall now cut each of them in two. At one stroke they will lose their strength and also become more profitable to us, owing to the increase in their number")[2] is followed by utter disaster and disappointment. The plan does not really work out, and the fantasy of complementarity is the very form of this failure and disaster. Each of the halves

> longed for its own other half, and so they would throw their arms about each other, weaving themselves together, wanting to grow together. In that condition they would die from hunger and general idleness, because they would not do anything apart from each other. Whenever one of the halves died and one was left, the one that was left still sought another and wove itself together with that. Sometimes the half he met came from a woman, as we'd call her now, sometimes it came from a man; either way, they kept on dying. (Plato 1997, p. 474 [191b])

In view of this strange and deplorable development, the gods decided to intervene once more, on a rather different level. Although it might seem a minor intervention in relation to the first one, this second intervention is in fact much more radical in its implications for the nature of the human race, since it is with it that sexuality, sexual reproduction, and sexual satisfaction are introduced to human beings for the first time. The former "sexes" were not exactly sexual in the usual meaning of the term; they had their genitals on the outside (as well as their faces) and they cast seed and made children, not in one another, but in the ground, "like cicadas." And this is where Zeus cut with his second intervention. He moved their genitals round to the front, and invented "interior reproduction" and its essential by-product: a satisfaction that serves no purpose but itself. The idea behind all this is described in a very matter-of-fact way:

> so that, when a man embraced a woman, he would cast his seed and they would have children; but when male embraced male, they would at least have the satisfaction of intercourse, after which they could stop embracing, return to their jobs, and look after their needs in life. (Plato 1997, p. 474 [191c–d])

There we have it: not very much is needed, a little surplus, unexpected, additional satisfaction ("enjoyment *ex machina*"), and people can return to their normal business, instead of embracing each other to death. Although from our cultural standpoint the quote fails to mention "heterosexual" enjoyment apart from the aim of reproduction, we still get a clear enough picture of where all this is heading: towards some relatively independent "satisfaction of intercourse," as Plato says through the mouth of Aristophanes.

Although after this interlude on sexuation Aristophanes immediately resumes his talk about love and desire being founded in the longing for our other lost half, this curious detail deserves our attention.

The transfer of genitals (cutting them off and attaching, fixing them in another place) does indeed seem to introduce a supplementary factor into the destiny of splitting, as well as into the perspective of complementarity and the desired fusion of two into One. This supplementary factor—let us call it "factor x"—is very much and very intimately related to what I call the comic object. On the most general level, this "factor x" is a factor of a supplementary satisfaction (satisfaction that does not correspond to, and is not a complement of, any need or demand). It is enjoyment as (originally) surplus-enjoyment (enjoyment as something that does not simply spring from, or originate in, the body). In the perspective of halves desperately searching for their other halves (and, upon finding them, no less desperately longing to grow together with them), in this perspective our "factor x" could be described as follows: not only do we not get what we are searching and longing for, on top of that we get something we haven't even asked for (and something which only further complicates things). The crucial point here is precisely that we are not dealing simply with the logic of compensation, which is always based on some kind of equivalence. What we get is the equivalent of nothing; it is, strictly speaking, a heteronomous addition, a supplement that brings with it a logic of its own. This logic is added to the previous one; it crosses it and places human beings, so to speak, at the crossroads or junction of two different chains of causality. All things considered, it is clear that sexual intercourse (and satisfaction) can only be an obstacle, an obstructive element, to the supposed organic merger or fusion that remains on the horizon as longing. It is an addition, an independent and self-standing element, operating on a local level, which cannot fail to be superfluous, redundant, uncalled-for from the perspective of a spherical whole. We could also say that the fixing of the genitals is not only that which enables some kind of relationship between the two, but also and at the same time that which "*comes between*" the two, and the logic of which is—most literally—at odds with the logic of unification and fusion. (Of course this is precisely the incongruity that can give power to the fantasies of harmonious and total love or devotion which demand or presuppose the exclusion of sexuality; these fantasies forget that love itself emerges *inside* this very incongruity, and that the elimination of sexuality also amputates love—it amputates it at the very point where the two logics cross each other.)

If we thus try to conceptually evaluate and grasp this aspect of Aristophanes' speech, we should say that it is only this second cut ("moving the genitals around") that brings us to the split in the strict sense of the term: that is to say, a split which is something other than simply halving or bisecting. It is a separation or a split that also adds or attaches to each "half" something that (locally and indirectly) links them together, while at the same time making them (relatively) independent (so that they can go about their business and take care of themselves). The genital organ is fixed on top of the beloved object, so to speak, on top of the two halves, superimposed on them. This curious detail did not, of course, escape Lacan, who comments on it in the seminar on *Transference* and points out precisely its link with comedy:

> This is unique and stunning in Plato's writing—the possibility of love appeasement is handed over to something that has an indisputable relationship, to say the least, with an operation performed on the subject of genitals. . . . This does not simply mean that the genital organ appears here as both the possibility of the cut and as junction with the

loved object, but that in relation to the latter it literally appears as su-perimposed. . . . How can one not be amazed by the fact that here, for the first and only time, in a speech about a very serious matter, love, Plato brings into play the sexual organ as such?

This fact confirms what I told you about the essential driving force of the comical, namely that it ultimately always involves a reference to phallus. And it is no coincidence that it is Aristophanes who speaks of this. He is the only one who can do it. (Lacan 1991, pp. 115–116)

I can correct Lacan on only one point: the passage discussed is not the only one in Plato that brings into play the sexual organ as such.[3] We will return to the question of the phallus as the ultimate comic reference in a moment, but for the time being let us pursue a bit further the implications of this Platonic version of sexuation via the superimposition of sexual organs.

Why is it that only here does the split in the proper sense of the word appear, a split that is something other than bisection and in-volves a relative autonomy of the two terms, as well as a possible relationship between them? Because the split from the other, or in relation to the other, gets transformed into something which is above all a split in relation to oneself, to (the place of) one's own enjoyment, which belongs to us as constitutively dislocated. It belongs to us as something that is—to use Bergson's terms—lit-erally encrusted upon our organism and our lives. In this way Aristophanes' speech touches upon an aspect of the "human con-dition" that is doubly interesting from the psychoanalytic per-spective. It is interesting not only because of its obvious reference to the dimension of castration, but even more so because it puts the very notion of castration in a surprising perspective which catches the essence of this often misunderstood notion.

In Lacan, the concept of castration is in fact precisely that which constitutes the relationship between man and his enjoyment as a relationship of a constitutive "encrusting." Castration is this very cut into the supposedly immediate link between the subject (or the body) and enjoyment, yet a cut that comes in the form of an additional "appendix enjoyment"; it refers to the gap that sepa-rates the body, from within, from its enjoyment, and *at the same time* binds it to it. The usual misunderstanding generated by the notion of castration is that we automatically see in it only an operator of removing, of taking away, that is to say, an operator of lack. Yet the Lacanian revolution in relation to this notion consists precisely in his positing castration at the point of structural coincidence of a lack and of a surplus, a coincidence between "no more enjoyment" and "more enjoyment," a coincidence so elegantly expressed in the French term plus-de-jouir, which can have both meanings. In other words, the fact that the body is separated from its own enjoyment does not imply simply a painful loss or deprivation: the separation refers above all to the fact that enjoyment emerges as relatively autonomous, it emerges through an interval in relation to the one whose enjoyment it is. It is only because of this interval that enjoyment becomes enjoyment in the first place, and it is in this sense that Lacan declares castration to be the condition of enjoyment, such as we know it. Castration is not simply an amputation of enjoyment, but precisely its emergence in the form of an appendix, that is, in the form of something that belongs to the subject in an essential, yet not immediate way; something that belongs to the subject via a necessary interval. Castration is what introduces a gap into the very logic and dynamics of (human) enjoyment, a gap on account of which enjoyment never directly coincides with itself or with ourselves as its "bearers," but inevitably raises the question of how we relate to our own enjoyment. Or, in yet other terms: castration is the machina responsible for the status of enjoyment as essentially ex machina enjoyment.[4]

Castration is what gives enjoyment its relative autonomy, what accounts for its possible objectification (enjoyment as object) and for its possible detachability. That is to say: it explains why, as "id," enjoyment can walk away in any direction, why it can find and realize itself in the most unusual or the most usual activities. This also means that it is this relative autonomy of enjoyment that makes possible and opens up the space for what is colloquially referred to as the "fear of castration," that is, the fear of entirely losing control over this relatively independent part of our being. In other words, the empirical "fear of castration" is always-already a *consequence* of castration—only if something already appears as separable/detachable can we fear that it will be taken away from us. Let us think again of the examples given by Žižek (see note 4): if the insignia that put me, say, in the official role of judge be taken away from me, I can experience this as "symbolic castration." But strictly speaking this level is already secondary: in order for the power to be taken away from me in such a manner, it already has to exist as something that is not an organic part of myself, but belongs to me only through an interval, that is to say, as an appendix that is already the effect of symbolic castration. Similarly, the enjoyment is not an antipode of castration, but is related to it in a double, seemingly paradoxical way: it is what only first emerges and gets its status with castration, but also that which can itself be subjected to "castration" as loss. Enjoyment is an annex of castration, but at the same time it appears precisely as the realm where we can lose control over enjoyment.

With the definition of enjoyment as essentially "encrusted" upon us, we touch on a very significant source of comedy at work in the fundamental human condition as determined by such (dis)location of enjoyment. The latter is at the origin of all those further dislocations and metonymic displacements that are so striking in analysis (as symptoms), and are so often used as material for comedy. The Miser Harpagon's treasure chest (as the object through which and only through which the hero can find any satisfaction) is an emblematic example of such metonymic dislocation of enjoyment, on the basis of its fundamental, constitutive dislocation, detachability, and relative autonomy. If comedy stages this via extreme, extravagant cases and situations, this does not by any means imply that these cases are aberrations, examples of abnormal as opposed to normal human functioning. Harpagon is not the quintessence of a possible perversion of human nature, he is the quintessence of this nature itself. Comedy is not a deviation from the norm, or its reversal, but its radicalization; it is a procedure that carries the (human) norm itself to its extreme point; it produces and displays the constitutive excess and extremity of the norm itself. The human norm is a fundamental dislocation of enjoyment, its potential objectification, detachability, independence, mobility (as fixation in another place). Strong, distinctive comic characters are always two things at the same time: they are the ones who enjoy (their symptom—whatever it is), and it is precisely because of this that they are also radically exposed, since whatever they enjoy is lying out there, for everyone to come across and stumble against.

This brings us once again to the question of the "invulnerability" of comic characters and the indestructibility of their happiness. How is it that whatever finally happens to the precious object of their obsession, even if they lost it irretrievably, they do not seem to be hopelessly crushed by this loss? This trait of comedy is usually explained by the theory of insignificance: comedy is made up of trivialities and trivial situations, and what the comic character eventually loses was insignificant, ridiculous, and trivial to begin with. This theory is simply untenable: there is a great deal of comic and tragic ("serious") material that directly contradicts it. The same passions that are the subject of comedy (love, jealousy, greed, ambition, and so on) can also be subjects of tragedy or of serious drama.

A very good example is Murnau's film *The Last Man*: the whole drama of this film, which is by no means a comedy, revolves around a uniform. An elderly man who has worked all his life as a hotel porter gets assigned to another, less distinguished job (cleaning), and is no longer allowed to wear his nice uniform. But since his status as a man at home and in the entire (poor) neighborhood where he lives depends on this ornate uniform (which he proudly used to wear to work and back), he cannot bear to lose it. So he goes through some complicated arrangements in order to be able to keep wearing the uniform on his way to and home from work (slipping out of it and hiding it just before he reaches the hotel). . . . So a man has lost his uniform. A rather trivial and insignificant loss, we might say. Yet *The Last Man* is an extremely sad and moving film, during which nobody doubts for a second that with the uniform the old man loses something essential: the very thing, the only thing, through which he existed as something (in the Symbolic). This same theme could, of course, be shot as a comedy; yet the difference would surely not be in the hero's less serious attachment to his uniform—rather, the contrary. What, then, is the difference?

It is not wrong to say that the difference lies in the perspective, yet we should be more specific; so let us try to approach the question from the following angle. Both the "tragic"[5] and "comic" rendering of the story would revolve around some trait that is insignificant in itself, yet becomes a pivotal point of someone's existence or destiny. A tragic story will usually show us how this happened (that is, provide a narrative explaining the circumstances of this short circuit) and, above all, narrate the individual destiny that follows. It will show us an exemplary and convincing case of how an insignificant thing like an item of clothing can become, in certain circumstances in the symbolic universe of the hero, most intimately connected with this hero's whole being; it will show us how the stripping off of his uniform can be experienced by the hero only as the stripping off of his being.

In the comic rendering of such a theme, on the other hand, the emphasis is not on *how* this general functioning of the Symbolic can affect the particular human being, but on the fact that *it does so*, and that it does so all the time. The emphasis is on the (repeated) display of this functioning, in all its oddity, not on the existential experience, feelings, and so on that it can produce in a particular human destiny. Human nature, as generated by the very intersection of the physiological and the symbolic, the biological and the cultural, has its own curious way of functioning, as well as its own way of being affected by its functioning. Comedy focuses on the former, and tragedy (or "serious drama") mostly on the latter. Comic characters are not individuals caught in a certain symbolic structure, following it, defying it, resisting it, and pointing out, through their particular destiny, its impasses and problematic points. This description is more suitable for tragic or "serious" heroes. Comic characters, on the other hand, are not subjects as opposed to the structure, they are subjectivized points of the structure itself. They are the sensitive, problematic points of the structure running wild, and running around on their own—that is, independently of the rest of the structure. This is why exaggeration and intensification are such important comic techniques.

We have a few very nice examples of this in Chaplin's *Modern Times*. For instance, in the factory scene when Charlie, after he has been performing the same gesture of fastening a screw for hours, cannot stop repeating this operation, but runs instead after everything that looks like a screw and attempts to fasten it with his spanner. To see this simply as a case of an illustration of how a poor worker ("subject") is turning into a machine would be to miss a crucial comic dimension of the scene. What we are shown rather, is a machine becoming a man in the figure of Charlie—that is to say, a machine "losing" it and starting to develop subjective tics (a beautiful blonde comes along with two buttons attached to the back of her skirt, and Charlie chases after her in an attempt to "screw" the buttons; then he runs out of the factory building and attempts to "screw" a phallic hydrant until it starts spurting water; then a heavier lady comes along, with two large buttons on the jacket covering her big bosom, and of course he wants to "screw" them . . .). The other great factory scene, the scene with the feeding machine, might seem to contradict our thesis. Here Charlie is not a subjective prolongation in which the structural machinery runs wild, but is reduced to a helpless object fed at the "will" of the machine and then, when the latter runs wild (loses a few screws, we might say), utterly subjected to its dysfunctional raging. But here also things are more interesting. At the beginning of the scene, Charlie is literally incorporated into the machine, and then the more he becomes a helpless toy in the "hands" of the feeding machine, the more the machine becomes Charlie. The machine itself starts behaving like a comic character, systematically missing the objective of its performance, right up to the obligatory cake it stuffs into Charlie's face. (And of course, Chaplin did in fact operate the feeding machine himself all the way through the shooting of this scene . . .).

I said above that comic strategies focus on displaying the functioning of symbolic structures (both on the fundamental, constitutive level and on the level of particular, culturally determined symbolic practices). This accounts for a certain "scientific" impression that comedies often give, even when they contain the most common "vulgar" situations. "Distance" is the word usually used to describe the comic approach. Yet this distance is not, as it is often held to be, a condition of comedy, but its inherent effect. It is the effect of the comic shift of perspective.

As a rule, comic characters do not invite the identification of the spectators, but instead do their best to divert it. What does this diversion involve? The essence of (symbolic) identification lies in what it allows us not to know about ourselves. We identify with a certain trait ("Master-Signifier"), and the relation of this trait to our singular mode of enjoyment—a relation that sustains the identification—remains unconscious. This is how we could write the formula of identification: $\frac{S_1}{a}$ with the object a below the bar above which we have the Master-Signifier. In other words, in order for the identification to be operative, the very joint between the (Master-) Signifier and enjoyment attached to the signifier (as its other side) has to remain hidden. I must be very precise here: I am not saying that the enjoyment attached to the signifier (as its other side) has to remain a secret, and that displaying it would break the spell of the identification. This is not necessary at all, as we have already seen in Part I: displaying the obscene, enjoying part of the master (or of any subject existing as a symbolic entity) is not enough to constitute comedy proper—which is to say, precisely, that it is not enough to break the spell of identification. And if we stop here for a moment, and take a broader perspective, we cannot fail to notice that a public display of (everybody's) enjoyment has become a privileged mode of contemporary mastery. "Look at them/us enjoying!" is the contemporary formula that is not meant to shame anyone,[6] or demean a public authority, but to consolidate it. There is nothing subversive in this reversal, which can be written as $\frac{a}{S_1}$. The Master-Signifier is the truth and the support of this willingly displayed enjoyment, and that is precisely why people stand in line to be able to do it: because by displaying it, they display their belonging to the (same) Master-Signifier, they display their belonging to the order of power.

So if there is nothing subversive or particularly comical in this kind of reversal of (the positions of) S_1 and a, if displaying the other, enjoying side of the Master-Signifier is not enough to break its spell, what could be? The answer is very precise: what can achieve this is an operation that locates with precision, and displays, the singular point of junction of the two elements. What really needs to remain hidden for any different form of mastery to function is not simply this or that (latent) content, this or that enjoyment, but the point of the constitutive linkage of S_1 and a, their *articulation* (to use the French term for joint), the very point where they are "encrusted" onto each other. To show the point of their *articulation* is to produce the effect of their disarticulation, disjunction. This could, of course, be related to our discussion of the functioning of jokes and of comic sequences. At the end of the joke, a Master-Signifier sutures its narrative and semantic field in a surprising manner: it "miraculously" produces a new meaning, bound up with a certain amount of pleasure. The new meaning remains fixed at the end of the joke (or it fixes this joke), and the pleasure is consummated in laughter. This mechanism is what constitutes all the ambiguity of joking in relation to mastery. Because it is produced right before our eyes, the joint of S_1 and a is clearly visible, and in this sense it counteracts the grip of mastery. Yet at the same time, and being—both literally and figuratively—the last word of the joke, the Master-Signifier is triumphantly affirmed: pleasure (laughter) confirms it in its mastery. We could say that the mechanism of the production of the joke ($S_1 \rightarrow a$) gets obfuscated in its final reinstalling the order of identification ($\frac{S_1}{a}$). A comic sequence, on the other hand, provides a setting for a more extensive display of the joint between the two elements. In our Oval Office example we could see this in each of the two protagonists insisting on his or her Master-Signifier (who–Hu): "who" is the signifier that decides meaning in George's reading of the story; "Hu" in Condi's. At the same time, they constitute each other's a: "who" is the laughable sense-in-nonsense of "Hu" as the Master-Signifier; "Hu" is the laughable sense-in-nonsense of "who" in the role of Master-Signifier. Via this double play (reinforced by newly occurring elements—Yes, sir/Yassir . . .), the point of junction between S_1 and a, their emerging from each other, is the very texture of the dialogue, the stuff it is made of, and not—as in the case of jokes—its underlying mechanism, perceptible only for a split second when the turn is produced. In this perspective, a comic sequence is like the glove of a joke turned inside out.

WOZU PHALLUS IN DÜRFTIGER ZEIT?

In my discussion of Aristophanes' myth in the *Symposium*, I introduced something like "full frontal castration" (to paraphrase Monty Python's "full frontal nudity") as the pivotal point of the structure of comedy, provided that we understand castration as the gap that at the same time separates the subject from and links her to her enjoyment and/or symbolic function.

This brings us to what is perhaps one of the most controversial points of Lacanian (or, more generally, psychoanalytic) theory today. If this is all about the inherent gap or noncoincidence, why not call it just that? Why call it "castration," with an explicit reference to the male organ? Lacan insists on the term castration, although what he means by it is very often misunderstood. The key to his argument is, first, that he calls the phallus the signifier of castration (and not, perhaps, the signifier of its opposite: of some full enjoyment, symbol of fecundity, or something of that kind). However, in understanding this we do not get very far if we simply keep repeating that the "phallus" is a symbolic function, and that it has nothing to do with the penis. For we can then repeat the same question as before: why, then, call this purely symbolic function the "phallus" (and not, for instance, the "gapus")? In all his complex elaboration of the phallic function as symbolic, it never crossed Lacan's mind to say something like: "But in the end, it doesn't really matter what one calls it." When he insists that the phallus is the signifier of castration, Lacan presses the following question: Why is it that this anatomical peculiarity of human males can and *does* function in human relationships, and for both sexes, as a signifier of castration (in the Lacanian sense of the term)? His answer to this might seem rather trivial, yet in all its trivial realism it makes a lot of conceptual sense. With its very anatomical peculiarity, the male organ quite obviously suggests (and displays) the following features: a relative autonomy of enjoyment (with, among other things, its not-always-predictable ups and downs); its local—or at least localizable—nature (the interval between the body and enjoyment); and the status of enjoyment as something that can be excluded, detached, or attached, annexed.[7] These are precisely the features Lacan associates with castration. To put it very bluntly: in the case of the male organ, we can see very clearly what comes between a man and his enjoyment—but also what comes between a woman and her enjoyment. By this I mean nothing but the fact that a woman's relationship to her enjoyment is also not simply an organic, immediate relationship, but involves a gap that sustains its possibility through its very impossibility. Contrary to what it might seem to be the case, the error of the claims about feminine enjoyment as immediate is most obvious precisely if we consider certain cases of feminine enjoyment that can strike us as most "organic" or "physical." Consider the classic hysterical symptoms which usually take the form of some kind of physical dysfunction. If we think about the flexibility of these symptoms, how they seem to be uncannily able to "decide" which part of the body will "take on" the impasse of enjoyment and "speak for it," we can perhaps get a clearer picture of the interval or gap that separates, from the inside, human enjoyment from the body that bears it. Lacan's point is that this is true for both sexes, and the phallus functions as the signifier of this interval for both sexes, whereas sexual difference is defined by the mode of the relationship that the subject assumes in respect to this signifier.

It would be difficult to avoid mentioning, in this context, that this is precisely the point where Otto Weininger slipped: he slipped on the fantasy of female enjoyment as noncastrated. The following passage is very eloquent in this respect, especially against the background of our former discussion:

> Woman is *only* sexual, man is *also* sexual. . . . In man, there are only a
> few body parts where he can be sexually aroused, and even these are
> strictly determined as to their *location*. In woman, sexuality spreads
> around her entire body, wherever you touch her, it excites her. . . .
> Since in man sexuality is only an appendix and is far from being
> everything, for men the sexuality can be psychologically distin-
> guished (separated) from the background, and he can *become aware*
> of it. . . . In woman, sexuality cannot be reflected against a non-sexual

area, since it doesn't occur in temporally limited outbursts, nor is there an anatomic organ where it could be locally seen already from the outside. (Weininger 1993, pp. 78–79)

It would be difficult to spell out the connection between the phallus and castration more clear: since woman does not have the phallus, she does not know castration, which is why her relation to enjoyment is immediate—it is all-embracing, and saturates everything. What is lacking is the cut ("separat[ion] from the background"), which, and only which, introduces a reflexive relation towards enjoyment, an awareness or consciousness which can never be immediate, but requires a certain distance or gap. From there it follows (for Weininger) that women do not have consciousness in the strict meaning of the word, and that they are not really capable of thinking. We can see very clearly how this fantasy of female enjoyment (as noncastrated) is based upon the apparent absence of visible, anatomical physical signs of detachability of enjoyment: since in the case of woman we cannot think of enjoyment (or *see* it) as excluded/excludable, she is "obviously" drawn and sunk into it entirely. Psychoanalysis (especially Lacanian) intervenes precisely at the point of this imaginarization of the sexual difference (its "metaphysics"): castration (in the sense described above) is a universal feature, and if it plays an important role in the difference between the sexes, it does so precisely as their common point, the point of their intersection.

So what is the crucial difference between Weininger and Lacan? For Weininger, the phallus, as an anatomical peculiarity of males, is a direct proof and expression of castration. In this perspective the phallus is not a signifier, it is not a symbolic function; rather, it is the anatomical condition of possibility of the Symbolic. Those who do not "have it" are not equipped to qualify as beings of the Symbolic; they are sunk into the immediacy of enjoyment, without being able to have a reflective relation to it. What Lacan does, on the other hand, is to reverse the order of this argument: the phallus, as anatomical peculiarity, becomes significant against the (preexisting) background of the Symbolic, the nodal point of which it comes to incarnate. In this way, far from sustaining the fascination with the phallus, Lacan offers an explanation of why this anatomical peculiarity has been able to function as a vehicle of some deeper meaning, and of all the metaphysics of the "other sex" which has so profoundly marked, throughout history, the discourse on women—because it relied upon the imaginary register, on whose screen the anatomical feature is transposed and transfixed into a Mystery of Essence. What Lacan discovered, and uncovered, was this unspeakable or never-spoken-of point, where a certain symbolic impasse or difficulty (which springs from the fact that we are beings of language, and that it is *precisely this fact* that introduces a constitutive split between the body and enjoyment) is linked to a specific image of localized human enjoyment—the phallus—which acquires the aura of a sublime Mystery *precisely against the background of and because of that symbolic impasse.*

In its *imaginary* function, the phallus is the veil that screens the traumatic point of linkage, the "impossible" joint between the Symbolic and the somatic. Or, even more precisely, in its imaginary dimension of Potency incorporated, the phallus veils and sustains the very "impotence" and impossibility (that is, the eternal difficulty) of the joint in question. This is also to say that it veils the point of anchorage of the phallic function (as symbolic) in the human body. In the imaginary register, the phallus is put up as the ultimate veil of castration—the position from which it draws its power to *fascinate.* "You want to see? Look at This (and you won't feel the need to look any further)!"

Insofar as this linkage is not specified and spelled out, it situates the phallus within the field where impossibility is combined with necessity—the configuration that Lacan very subtly formulates as: it doesn't stop not being written. Since it cannot be written, it doesn't stop not being written, it doesn't stop, it persists as necessary in its very impossibility. And it is precisely at this point that psychoanalysis intervenes; this is why Lacan takes a considerable feminist pride in relation to his own contribution to the dethroning of the phallus. By spelling out the link between the traditionally almighty phallus (which, by the way, functioned symbolically, and as a symbolic power, long before Lacan came along) to an anatomical peculiarity, he (and psychoanalysis) made a crucial contribution to the removal of the phallus from the mode of necessity to that of contingency. The phallus has stopped not being written.

> Analysis presumes that desire is inscribed on the basis of a corporal contingency. Let me remind you what I base this term "contingency" on. The phallus . . . analytic experience stops not writing it. It is in this "stops not being written" [*cesse de ne pas s'écrire*] that resides the apex of what I have called contingency. . . . Because of this, the apparent necessity of the phallic function turns out to be mere contingency. . . . It is only as contingency that, thanks to psychoanalysis, the phallus, reserved in ancient times to the Mysteries, has stopped not being written. Nothing more. It has not entered into the "doesn't stop," that is, into the field on which depend necessity, on the one hand, and impossibility. (Lacan 1998, p. 94)

Psychoanalysis has thus spoken out about the link on account of which an anatomical peculiarity, because of the symbolic deadlock or impasse whose place it comes to occupy, acquires an exceptional symbolic significance. It is through this gesture, which discloses the interval that separates and links the symbolic and the anatomical (the interval that allows, precisely, for their articulation) that a crucial knowledge is produced: the knowledge that makes it impossible to keep considering anatomy as our destiny.

This is not to say, however, that the symbolic impasse on whose account the phallus acquires its significance is not real, or that it can simply be eliminated. But what exactly is this (universal) impasse that psychoanalysis calls castration? As I have already suggested from several different angles, it could be conceived as the very point of junction of the organic and the symbolic, their joint, their *articulation*. There is something about this joint that is never linear, or nonproblematic, but involves instead a jump and, as I formulated it in Part I, a leak. The fact that psychoanalysis links this point with sexuality and calls its specific effect "castration" is essential, and at the same time constitutes the side of psychoanalysis that is most often attacked—not only by "conservative" moralists, but even more so by "liberal" culturalists. The "sexual reductionism" of psychoanalysis and its supposedly "obvious phallocentrism" are two objections that miss their mark by such a long way that their insistence is definitely symptomatic. It is symptomatic because it involves a radical disavowal of what was really ground-breaking in the psychoanalytic discovery of sexuality. Psychoanalysis did not focus on sexuality, bring it to light, and try to explain (more or less) everything by it. This perspective presupposes that sexuality is a well-established (albeit veiled by considerations of modesty) realm of human nature, nonproblematic in itself, but problematic in its relationship to other human dimensions, especially to culture and its restraints. What Freud actually discovered, on the contrary, was that sexuality was a problem in itself, a question, not a solution (to problems and questions of humanity); far from being something with which one could explain other different human phenomena, it needs an explanation itself.

Freud's point was not that sexuality is a natural realm of human life which created problems only in its encounter with cultural codes and restraints; his crucial point was that human sexuality is the very encounter between "nature" and "culture," that it is the name of their always difficult, problematic, and erratic junction. This junction is the site of sexuation in the strict meaning of the word. What does this tell us? Human sexuality is not sexual simply because it includes the sexual organs (or organs of reproduction). Rather, there is something in the very constitution of human nature that, so to speak, sexualizes sexual activity itself, endows it with a surplus-investment (one could also say that it sexualizes the activity of reproduction). This point might seem paradoxical, but if we think of what distinguishes human sexuality from, let us say, animal or vegetable sexuality—is it not precisely the fact that human sexuality is sexualized (which could also be put in a punch line like: "Sex is sexy")? This constitutive redoubling of sexuality is what makes it always-already dislocated not only in respect to its reproductive purpose, but also and above all in respect to itself. The moment we try to provide a clear definition of sexual activity, we run into trouble. We run into trouble because human sexuality is ridden with this paradox: the further sex departs from the "pure" copulating movement (that is to say, the wider the range of elements it includes in its activity), the more sexual it becomes. Sexuality gets sexualized precisely in this constitutive interval that separates it from itself. Nothing could be further from psychoanalysis than the simplistic claim that sexuality has its natural place in human life, that this place should be acknowledged, and sexuality given a proper consideration alongside other human activities. The central point of Freud's discovery was precisely that there is no "natural" or preestablished place of human sexuality; that it is constitutively out-of-it-place, fragmented, and dispersed; that is exists only in deviations from "itself" or its supposed natural object; and that sexuality is nothing but this "out-of-placeness" of its constitutive satisfaction. In other words, Freud's fundamental move was to desubstantialize sexuality: the sexual is not a substance to be properly described and circumscribed, it is the very impossibility of its own circumscription or delimitation. It can neither be completely separated from biological, organic needs and functions (since it originates within their realm, it starts off by inhabiting them), nor simply reduced to them. The sexual is not a separate domain of human activity or life, and this is precisely why it can inhabit all the domains of human life.[8]

It is because this paradoxical joint between the biological body and the Symbolic is inherently sexual (in the sense that it constitutes the generative source of human sexuality) that its effect is called castration. The "phallic signifier" as the signifier of castration (also referred to as the signifier of lack) is, one could say, the signifier of the missing link between the biological and the Symbolic (or between nature and culture) as the generic point of sexuation. This is why psychoanalysis must resist the conciliatory "philosophical"

attempt to replace the term castration with something more neutral, like the description of the human condition as essentially paradoxical, limited, finite, vulnerable. . . . For this is nothing but a
remystification of something which psychoanalysis has already
demystified. The cultural neutralization of the concept of castration (into more or less pathetic slogans about human limitations)
is part of the very same tradition that was inaugurated by Jung in
relation to Freud. That is to say: the discovery of the real impasse
inherent to human sexuality, as well as the operating of this impasse in the present actuality of each and every subject (where its
destiny is being decided, again and again), is translated into this
or that cultural archetype, which is certain to endow the impasse
in question with a dignified patina, and cover it with the mist of a
respectful Mystery. If anything, this—not the term phallic signifier—is an emphatic gesture of "phallicization." it would be very
wrong to think that so-called phallocentrism could be countered
by a politically correct restriction regarding the use of the term
phallus. As history makes more than clear, phallocentrism can
work splendidly, and much better, if the phallus is not directly
named, but reserved for Mysteries. And we should not forget that
it was only with the advent of psychoanalysis that talk about phallocentrism really took off in the first place.

Thus those who reproach (Freudian–Lacanian) psychoanalysis
with phallocentrism reveal a spectacular misapprehension of the
fundamental psychoanalytic act. By using the name phallic signifier and by insisting on the signifying, symbolic function of the
phallus, Lacan is by no means idealizing—and thus "rescuing"—
a male anatomical peculiarity, promoting it into an ultimate reference of human reality. His gesture is exactly the opposite: onto the
very ground where, throughout the centuries, the phallus has had
only a cultural signification—that is to say, (religious, as well as
other) rituals and symbolic practices encapsulating the Mystery
of Man and dictating the hierarchic structures of his universe as
emanating directly from this supreme Mystery—onto this very
ground steps Lacan, and Freud before him, to say: Surprise, sur-

prise—the Mystery is none other than the phallus, and it draws its power from the symbolic workings of castration. To call the signifier of castration the "phallic signifier" implies both a real and a conceptual desublimation of the mystery of the Phallus. It is not a culturalization of the real phallus in a quasi-neutral symbol but, rather, a *realization* of its cultural significance and meaning— that is to say, an act of reattaching this significance to the piece of the Real whose veiling has produced the effects of the sublime Meaning.

And could we not say that the human practice which, in its own way, has always already pointed its finger at precisely such links between the "highest" and the "lowest," between the purely spiritual/symbolic and the materially anatomically obscene, is precisely comedy?

To a great extent, human society and culture are constructed around what we could briefly call "respect for castration." The manners we teach our children (don't stare, don't point, don't talk back, respect the elderly, don't make fun of people who seem strange to you) are all modes of respect for castration. They introduce and demand a certain distance, thus making it possible for us not to walk on each other's enjoyment, if this can be avoided. The veil of respect and the blush of shame usually conceal the fact that there is nothing behind them; yet this does not mean that this "behind" can simply be eliminated with the proclamation that surface is everything, and "behind" is a mere metaphysical illusion. Comedy likes to transgress the rules and demands of respect. It also likes to unveil the veils, tear down the folding screens, and open the closets. Yet it does not usually claim directly that there is nothing behind. Rather the contrary: behind the veil there is always a naked bottom, behind the folding screen a scantily clad lady, and there is always, of course, a lover hidden in the closet. Comedy is in very great need of this double configuration. We could even say that in comedy, there is always something behind. Yet the comic point is that what is behind is—Surprise, surprise!—nothing but what we would expect (from the surface of things). Concerning the proverbial comic scene of the lover in the closet, Mladen Dolar has made an important point. Imagine *Othello*, the classic tragic masterpiece on the theme of jealousy—what would happen if Othello were in fact to find a lover in Desdemona's closet? The whole thing would immediately turn into a comedy, if not a farce (Dolar 2005a, p. 203).

In this context we could formulate a further important difference between comedy and tragedy. It is essential to tragedy that there is nothing behind, that the closet is empty; and it is precisely this nothing that becomes the space of the hero's infinite passion, which ultimately brings him down. The hero, be it Oedipus or Othello, is convinced that there is something behind. Yet what he finds behind the curtain is himself as *subject*, his own passion, and it is this confrontation that finally brings him down. On the other hand, what comedy puts in the place of this infinite passion is a finite, trivial object: instead of the abyssal negativity of the subject, it puts there its other, "objective," objectified side.

This gesture desublimates this dimension or the space of "the behind," but *at the same time it preserves* it. Comedy always materializes and gives a body to what can otherwise appear as an unspeakable, infinite Mystery of the other scene. Of course there is always something behind. You want to see? Watch this! Of course there is always a lover in the closet and a naked bottom under the skirt. What else did you expect? The key is precisely in the fact that in comedy we are usually surprised by things and events that we, at least roughly, expect. And we could even say that what often surprises us is precisely that there is no particular surprise—that what is behind is indeed precisely this: Here it would be difficult to resist quoting one more time Groucho Marx's famous line: *He may look like an idiot and talk like an idiot, but don't let that fool you. He really is an idiot.* Thus, the point is not simply that surface is everything: of course it is, but this cannot be said or shown directly. Comedy needs and plays upon the duality of appearance and truth, of surface and depth. But it does so in a way which, at some precise point, links the two, or in a way that endows the subject's infinite passion with the form of a concrete—and thus necessarily "banal"—object (which is behind). The mental experiment we carried out above with *Othello* can also be carried out in the opposite direction—say in the case of Molière's *L'Avare/ The Miser*. Considering the passion that dominates the main character, Harpagon could also have been a tragic hero: avarice, this sole motor of his existence, drives him far beyond the pleasure principle, and threatens to ruin his life as well as the lives of those close to him. But in comedy this passion has a very concrete shape and size: ten thousand silver coins, Harpagon's treasure, buried in the garden, where he regularly visits it and counts it. What is funny in this play is not simply Harpagon's idolatry of money, but above all the incarnation of the subject's finite passion in this countable object. However, that does not make Harpagon's passion any less real and infinite—and this is what makes it comical. It is comical because, bound to this object, it is at the same time real, infinite, and desublimated.

This is precisely how comedy helps us to understand a crucial dimension of the Lacanian notion of castration: castration is not simply a lack (which would be the origin of an infinite desire and passion), it always comes in this or that concrete form—for instance, the form of a lover in the closet, or the form of ten thousand silver coins.

Concluding Remarks

Let us now return to the question of the phallus and comedy. If Lacan did in fact point to the link between the phallus (or its appearance) and an essential dimension of comedy, and comment on it,[9] he did not invent this link. Rather, we are discussing something that has been pointed out by virtually all theoreticians and historians of comedy, especially those concerned with its origins and beginnings. At the beginning of this Appendix, I quoted the Aristotelian thesis about the origins of comedy as related to the ritual of performing "phallic songs." Phallic songs were sung during rituals honoring Dionysus. In these rituals the participants would march in procession, carrying a phallus of huge proportions made of animal skins, and singing obscene songs, full of ambiguous innuendo. This theory of the origins of comedy is widely accepted, and strongly corroborated by (documented) conventions of the staging of comedies in the early days: the actors often wore costumes to which big leather phalluses were attached, sometimes additionally highlighted by being painted, for example, in red (see Silk 2002, p. 8).

Of course, comedy has developed quite a bit, and in various different directions, since those ancient times. In modern comedy, the appearance of the phallus in person is somewhat rare, although by no means nonexistent. If we accept that there is indeed a strong phallic reference at the heart of comedy, even when the phallus itself is not so persistently displayed, we might relate it to the following considerations.

Perhaps the most important conceptual conclusion that may be drawn from the different points we have brought into our analysis is that in its specificity, comedy is essentially a genre of the copula. It is not simply a genre of the two, as I have also suggested—rather, the two, the redoubling and other different kinds of duality that are so prominent in comedy, are vehicles for exploring what is most central to comedy: the function and operation of the copula. We have already had the chance to note the long series of dualities or oppositions with which comedy plays and constructs. If some of them (like the Bergsonian couple mechanical/living) seem to come closer to capturing the essence of the comic opposition than others, it is because they come closest to rendering the opposition or duality that constitutes the very heart (hidden or not) of comedy. And this is the duality of life and the signifier; or, in other possible, more extensive formulations: of the biological and the symbolic, of nature and culture. This opposition is not simply one among others, nor do I want to claim its privilege simply because it is fundamental, and preexists all the others. Its singularity lies in the configuration of the *relationship* between the two terms involved in it, namely in the fact that their opposition comes from their essential overlapping, and their relationship from their fundamental nonrelationship. The human condition may be defined as the zone where the two realms overlap. Yet this formulation, although it is not false, can be strongly misleading, and wide open to religious readings of human beings as composed of two principles. Hence the crucial point is that what is at stake is not an overlapping of two already well-established entities, but an intersection which is generative of both sides that overlap in it. If psychoanalysis can help us to understand this, that is because one of its most important discoveries consisted in detecting precisely this kind of logic and dialectic: it focused on the points where the biological or somatic is already symbolic or cultural and where, at the same time, culture springs from the very impasses of the somatic functions which it tries to resolve (yet, while doing so, creates new ones). In other words, human beings are composed neither of the biological and the symbolic, nor of the physical and the metaphysical—the image of composition is misleading. Human beings are, rather, so many points where the difference between the two elements, as well as the two elements themselves as defined by this difference, are generated, and where the relationship between the two dimensions thus generated is being constantly negotiated.[10]

There is no "pure life" or "pure Symbolic" prior to this curious intersection. The generating point of the Symbolic is this paradoxical joint, and the Symbolic as a wholly independent, autonomous realm is something produced—it is produced at the periphery of the movement generated by the intersection, and retroactively affecting its own point of generation—its own "birth," so to speak. The nature of this intersection is such that we can precisely not see it as an intersection; we cannot put a finger on it and say: *Voilà*, it is here that "nature" is becoming "culture." This passage can be noticed and established only from the latter point, that is to say, from where it has already taken place. In other words, the double circular movement described corresponds in fact to the movement along the surface of the Möbius strip: we start, say, at an extreme point of one side, and without ever passing to the other side, we end up at an extreme point of it. This brings us back to the point—or, more exactly, two points—made in Part I of this discussion of comedy. First, what the topology of the Möbius strip reveals is that the missing link that structures our reality is not a missing link between two neighbor elements, the connection between which would thus be interrupted—instead, its very missing is the linkage between two neighbor elements; it is what makes it possible for them to "fit" into each other. Second, comedy forces this constitutive missing link to appear as something—not by trying to provide its own version of the (always fantasmatic) moment of the passage of one side into the other, but by producing a short circuit between two sides, and sustaining it ("playing with it") as a possible articulation of the impossible. It is here that comedy fully affirms itself as the genre of the copula that articulates together, in its specific way, the two heterogeneous dimensions of the same reality.

The phallus is the privileged signifier of this copula, precisely inasmuch as the latter exists only in the background of a missing link. This, I believe, is what accounts for its important role in comedy. To a certain extent at least, the significance of the phallus and the significance of comedy revolve around the same thing: the missing link between life and signifier. The phallus is the signifier of this missing link, yet its appearance in comedy is not simply in the form of the signifier. Rather, in comedy this signifier itself appears in the form of an object.

I should indeed stress that the phallus is by no means only a signifier. In human experience it appears in three different forms or dimensions: (1) As the signifier of castration, the signifier without the signified, the signifier of the very cut that marks human beings as constitutively dislocated in relation to themselves. (2) As an image, that is to say in the imaginary register of some dazzling fullness, veiling the lack at its core. (3) As a partial object (that is, one in the series of partial objects), which is as such also a real locus of enjoyment, and is already mediated by the cut of symbolic castration against the background of which it appears, yet the impediments of which it tends to escape at the same time—which is precisely where comedy comes in.

One could say that it is the destiny of the phallus in comedy that it can appear only as a comic object, that is to say, an object that materializes in itself the very contradictions of the Symbolic that produces it. Comedy thrives on these impasses as the very stuff of which the social fabric is made.

To define comedy as the genre of the copula is in fact to place it at the most sensitive and precarious point of this fabric, the point where it is being generated and regenerated, torn apart and fused together, solidified or transformed. This would explain, for example, why comedy has often thrived in moments of social crisis. The explanation according to which this is due to the fact that in order to survive in hard times, people need comedy and laughter, is inadequate, and does not cover the whole issue; or it should be formulated slightly differently and in more precise terms. It is a fact that keeping comedy going in critical situations can be a form of resistance, resistance to that tendency of completely reducing the subject(ivity), say, to a victimized "suffering flesh" or to some other all-absorbing determination—a tendency which usually accompanies critical situations and "hard times." The zone of subjectivity that comedy might thus help us preserve and sustain is, of course, fundamentally ambivalent. It could function as that distance that ultimately helps to sustain the very oppression of the given order or situation, because it makes it bearable and induces the illusion of an effective interior freedom. On the other hand, however, it is precisely a surplus, empty place of subjectivity that constitutes the playground of any possible change, and gets mobilized in this change. It is the production of this kind of subjectivized empty space that the movement of comedy is very good at.

Let me conclude with a few remarks concerning the paradoxical realism of comedy. As I have already pointed out, comedy involves a strange coincidence of realism (it is supposed to be more realistic and down-to-earth than, say, tragedy) and utter unrealism (defying all human and natural laws, and getting away with things that one would never get away with in "real life"). This unrealistic, "incredible" side of comedy is also related to its proverbial vitalism: a kind of undead, indestructible life, a persistence of something that keeps returning to its place no matter what. . . . I would suggest that it is precisely here, in this utterly unreasonable insistence, that we find the true realism of comedy, which is not the realism of the "reality principle," but that of some fundamental discrepancy as constitutive of human beings—a discrepancy which is not posited by comedy as painful or even tragic, but as surprisingly and funnily productive. One of the principal forms in which comedy illustrates this discrepancy is this very "unbelievable" persistence, which is very close to what Alain Badiou, in his book on Beckett and in relation to comedy, calls *l'increvable désir* (Badiou 1995, p. 75). We have already come across the term *increvable* in relation to Beckett, in Alfred Simon's description of the Beckettian hero ("*À defaut d'être immortel, il est increvable!*"—"He may not be immortal, but he's indestructible!"). Badiou relates the term to a specific aspect of comic desire: *l'increvable désir* refers to desire that will not die, or "snuff it." This is now I would put what is at stake here: Of course people die, suffer, find themselves in terrible predicaments with no way out. Comedy does not deny all this. What it does is add something else, something which is not simply a belief in the immortality of desire (or drive—*l'increvable désir* could in fact be a good definition of the drive), but refers to the fact—accessible in everyday experience—of the incongruence of the reality of desire and drive with all those (also quite factual) outlines that determine our supposedly realistic reality. The realism of comedy is the realism of this incongruence. In other words, by drawing on the structures of desire and drive, comedy does not preach that something of our life will or could go on living when we die; rather, it draws our attention to the fact that *something of our life lives on its own as we speak*, that is to say, at any moment of our life.

There is a great joke that could be called a comedy-joke, for it is precisely a joke about this fundamental illogic of comedy, which is very much the logic of the Real of human desire. The joke comes from the arsenal of the old Yugoslav-Bosnian jokes about Mujo and Haso. Since its logic is quite cross-cultural, I will risk an attempt at translating it.

Haso is describing to Mujo his adventures in the Sahara.

—I'm walking through the desert. Nothing but sand around me, not a living soul, absolutely nothing. . . . The sun burning in the sky, and my throat burning with thirst. Suddenly a lion appears in front of me. What to do, where to hide?—I climb a tree . . .

—Wait a minute, Mujo, you've just told me that there was nothing around but sand, so where did the tree come from?

—My dear Haso, you don't ask such questions when a lion appears! You run away and climb the first tree.

At stake here is by no means a disavowal of human reality and its limitations but, rather, a full recognition of the Real of human desire, able—if need be—effectively to climb a tree that is not there. Or to suddenly make a tree emerge in the middle of the desert.

INTRODUCTION

1. For a discussion of this last point, see Žižek 2006, pp. 170–174, 220–230.

PART I: THE CONCRETE UNIVERSAL

1. "The pure thoughts of the Beautiful and the Good thus display a comic spectacle: through their liberation from the opinion which contains both their specific determinateness as content and also their absolute determinateness . . . they become empty, and just for that reason the sport of mere opinion and the caprice of any chance individuality" (Hegel 1977, p. 452).

2. A poor man boasts about his good relationship with the rich Baron Rothschild, who treats him quite as an equal—quite "famillionairely."

3. There are, of course, comedies that have their main character's name as the title. *Borat* was a recent example. Yet if we think about it, "Borat" actually functions as a generic name (for crass prejudiced stupidity) or, more precisely, it functions as a short circuit between the generic and the individual. *Borat* is also a good example of the fact that comic characters are not simply represented by (different) actors, and that their link goes "beyond representation" in the usual sense of the term: it reminds us that it is by no means uncommon for comic characters (actors) to carry on with their "act" beyond the fictional framework (stage, movie) to which they belong. The promotion tour of *Borat* was done by Borat himself. This made it much more effective (and appropriate) than a promotion in which Sacha Baron Cohen talked about (t)his character, about how and why he created it, and thus posited himself as the subject behind Borat. On the other

hand, it is rather difficult to imagine, say, a promotion of a new production of *Hamlet* being done by Hamlet himself, that is to say, by the actor carrying on as Hamlet in the "outside" world.

4. This is what the Online Etymological Dictionary offers in the entry **wit:**

> "mental capacity," O.E. *wit*, more commonly *gewit*, from P.Gmc. **witjan* (cf. O.S. *wit*, O.N. *vit*, Dan. *vid*, Swed. *vet*, O.Fris. *wit*, O.H.G. *wizzi* "knowledge, understanding, intelligence mind," Ger. *Witz* "wit, witticism, joke," Goth. *unwiti* "ignorance"), from PIE **woid-/*weid-/*wid-* "to see," metaphorically "to know" (see vision). Related to O.E. *witan* "to know" (source of wit (v.)). Meaning "ability to make clever remarks in an amusing way" is first recorded 1542; that of "person of wit or learning" is from c. 1470. *Witticism* coined 1677, by Dryden. For nuances of usage, see *humor*.

5. This is a very important point: in relation to the judgment "God is man," the same analysis applies as to the judgment "substance is subject." On the latter, see the excellent and exhaustive analysis by Slavoj Žižek in *The Ticklish Subject* (Žižek 1999, pp. 70–103).

6. A different and very important dimension of creatureliness, which is also not without a possible relationship to comedy, has recently been described by Eric Santner in his excellent book *On Creaturely Life* (Santner 2006).

7. "Passage à l'art ali umetnost kot dejanje. Drugi del: sublimacija in ljubezen," *Problemi* 1–2/2000. See also Zupančič 2003, pp. 176–178.

8. Mladen Dolar develops this point beautifully in relation to the object-voice (see Dolar 2006).

9. For an excellent commentary on this point, and on Beckett in general, see Dolar 2005a. Here is Dolar's "translation" of *increvable*: "The dictionary offers 'to kick the bucket' as a trivial expression for dying, so could one say 'unbucketable'? Could one say 'unbeckettable'? He is not immortal, he just can't kick the bucket." (Ibid., p. 159.)

PART II: FIGURES OF COMEDY

1. All English translations of Molière are from Project Gutenberg (free electronic books): *www.gutenberg.org.*

2. See Dolar 2005a—not only for this point, but for an excellent study of the theme of the double in *Amphitryon* and in comedy in general.

3. I owe this example to Dolar, who discusses it in more detail; see Dolar 2005a.

4. Which is pronounced exactly like *les noms du père*, "the names of the father."

5. I should perhaps point out that this is precisely the tradition to which ultimately belongs a whole subgenre of the Hollywood comedies of the 1930s, that of "comedies of remarriage." The discrepancy between marriage and true love is transposed into an inner gap of the marriage itself, opened up in its redoubling. As Stanley Cavell has shown quite convincingly, these comedies are not simply a conservative attempt at saving the institution of marriage in crisis, but are in many respects much more subversive than the simplistic opposition between love and marriage. See Cavell 1981.

PART III: CONCEPTUALIZATIONS

1. We could even imagine a situation in which a body could clumsily fail to wear some elegant clothes properly, thus giving the impression of an inert thing in relation to a subtle garment.

2. Just think of the classic example of Heine's "Famillionaire" discussed by Freud (see Part I Note 2 above), or this example from the Marx Brothers' *Duck Soup*:

   TREASURY SECRETARY: Sir, you try my patience!
   FIREFLY (Groucho): Don't mind if I do. You must try mine sometime.

3. "Über die allmähliche Verfertigung der Gedanken beim Reden" (Kleist 1990), e406. For an excellent commentary on this, see Gailus 2006.

4. This notion appears in Freud's work on jokes (Freud 1976, p. 118), as well as in his "Three Essays on the Theory of Sexuality" (Freud 1977, p. 131). It was Joan Copjec who first drew my attention to this notion of an incentive bonus in Freud.

5. For more on this, see the chapter "On Love as Comedy" in Zupančič 2003.

6. See *Logiques des mondes* (Badiou 2006).

7. In this context, it might be worth recalling that before the invasion of Iraq the US intervention there was referred to by the Bush administration as, among other things, "bringing the capitalist revolution in Iraq."

8. This emphasis is very important in relation to what went on in Marxist debates (or debates on Marxism) concerning the notion of the "historic *necessity* of the proletarian revolution." For Marx indicates a fundamental difference in the status of necessity between past revolutions and the proletarian revolution. In brief: if it is true that all past revolutions "accomplished the task of their time," and were in this respect (but) agents, executors of a historic necessity (of socioeconomic development), this is no longer true of the proletarian revolution, or at least not in the same way. A revolution which can draw its poetry only from the future cannot be a

direct expression/consequence of a historic necessity; there is a difference, a nuance which could perhaps be formulated by stating that the necessity of the proletarian revolution is *ethical*.

9. Deleuze makes this claim very emphatically in the Introduction, but does
   not really return to it later—perhaps because the further he advances in
   establishing an immediate link between repetition and difference (repetition as operator of the difference, which—as one with being—is finally
   all there is), the more difficult it becomes to maintain its exceptional character.

10. "First, the *tyche*, which we have borrowed from Aristotle, who uses it in
    his search for cause. We have translated it as the encounter with the real.
    The real is beyond the *automaton*, the return, the coming-back, the insis-
    tence of the signs, by which we see ourselves governed by the pleasure
    principle. The real is that which always lies behind the *automaton*. . . ."
    (Lacan 1986, pp. 53–54.)

11. This point is also made by Lacan; see Lacan 1986, p. 63.

12. The explicitly comic tone that opens the play scene is not unrelated to
    what was said about the play scene itself: although the (re)presented
    events are tragic, and undoubtedly fit into the tragic structure of the play,
    there is also another aspect of the play that puts it in an intriguingly game-
    like perspective (including mechanical repetition).

13. This was the title of a very interesting conference held in Berlin in June
    2006 on the question of the links between the two genres.

(ESSENTIAL) APPENDIX: THE PHALLUS

1. Added to which are the famous hiccups that overcome Aristophanes the
   moment it is his turn to talk about love, so that he has to deliver his speech
   at a later point. Aristophanes' speech, when it comes, is quite literally "out
   of place."

2. See Plato 1997, pp. 473–474 (190d).

3. There is another, rather famous passage of this kind in *Timaeus*, in the last
   part of the discussion of the emergence of sexual desire and sexual difference. It is worth quoting in full:

   > And this explains why at the time the gods fashioned the desire for sexual
   > union, by constructing one ensouled living thing in us as well as another
   > one in women. This is how they made them in each case: There is [in a
   > man] a passage by which fluids exit from the body, where it receives the
   > liquid that has passed through the lungs down into the kidneys and on into
   > the bladder and expels it under pressure of air. From this passage they

bored a connecting one into the compacted marrow that runs from the head along the neck through the spine. This is in fact the marrow that we have previously called "seed." Now because it has soul in it and had now found a vent [to the outside], this marrow instilled a life-giving desire for emission right at the place of venting, and so produced the love of procreation. This is why, of course, the male genitals are unruly and self-willed, like an animal that will not be subject to reason and, driven crazy by its desires, seeks to overpower everything else. The very same causes operate in women. A woman's womb or uterus, as it is called, is a living thing within her with a desire for childbearing. Now when this remains unfruitful for an unreasonably long period of time, it is extremely frustrated and travels everywhere up and down her body. It blocks up her respiratory passages, and by not allowing her to breathe it throws her into extreme emergencies, and visits all sorts of other illnesses upon her until finally the woman's desire and the man's love bring them together. (Plato 1997, pp. 1289–1290 [91a–c])

As is well known, the last part of this passage was responsible for the original naming of hysteria (from *hystera*, uterus) and for its being considered, for a long time, an illness caused by a "wandering uterus," moving around within the body and causing difficulties in its various parts. As for the "male" part of the story, Plato's account provides an intriguing "explanation" of the paradoxical "conjunction of the high and the low," mentioned by Hegel apropos of the male organ. The "organ of pissing" gets its soul and its vent by an operation that connects the other end of its path to the ensouled marrow extending from the head, which now finds its way out through the same opening as urine. We also notice that in this passage sexuality is again presented as "superimposed" on human beings, as organism-within-organism, as life that lives as a parasite on life, so to speak.

4. We should be more precise and say that the concept of castration involves two registers of separation and of the exteriority of the interior. The first concerns enjoyment, the second concerns meaning (as symbolic meaning, related to the signifier). Since in our present discussion we are mostly dealing with the first, let us at least point to the second, concisely formulated by Slavoj Žižek in the following passage:

> So, what is symbolic castration, with the phallus as its signifier? One should begin by conceiving of the phallus as a signifier—which means what? From the traditional rituals of investiture, we know the objects that not only "symbolize" power, but put the subject who acquires them into the position of effectively *exercising* power. If a king holds in his hands the scepter and wears the crown, his words will be taken as the words of a king. Such insignia are external, not part of my nature: I don them; I wear them to exert power. As such, they "castrate" me: they introduce a gap between what I immediately am and the function that I exercise (i.e. I am never fully

at the level of my function). This is what the infamous "symbolic castration" means. Not "castration as symbolic, as just symbolically enacted" (in the sense in which we say that, when I am deprived of something, I am "symbolically castrated"), but the castration that occurs by the very fact of my being caught in the symbolic order, assuming a symbolic mandate. Castration is the very gap between what I immediately am and the symbolic mandate that confers on me this "authority.". . . And one has to think of the phallus not as the organ that immediately expresses the vital force of my being, my virility, and so forth but, precisely, as such an insignia, as a mask that I put on in the same way a king or a judge puts on his insignia— phallus is an "organ without a body" that I put on, which gets attached to my body, without ever becoming its "organic part," namely, forever sticking out as its incoherent, excessive supplement. (Žižek 2004, p. 87)

5. Here I leave aside the important differences between Murnau's film and tragedy proper, and use the term "tragic" in its less specific sense.

6. For more on this, see Miller 2006; Laurent 2006.

7. Compare:

Of course, it is not only the phallus that is present in sexual relations. However, what this organ has that is privileged is that in some way it is quite possible to isolate its *jouissance*. It is thinkable as excluded. To use violent words . . . it has, precisely, a property that, within the entire field of what constitutes sexual equipment, we may consider to be very local, very exceptional. There is not, in effect, a very large number of animals for whom the decisive organ for copulation is something as isolatable in its functions of tumescence and detumescence, determining a perfectly definable curve, called orgasmic—once it's over, it's over. (Lacan 2007, p. 75)

This citation is from 1970, but already as early as 1958 Lacan makes a similar point in his écrit "The Signification of Phallus":

One could say that this signifier is chosen as the most salient of what can be grasped in sexual intercourse [*copulation*] as real, as well as the most symbolic, in the literal (typographical) sense of the term, since it is equivalent in intercourse to the (logical) copula. One could also say that, by virtue of its turgidity, it is the image of the vital flow as it is transmitted in generation. (Lacan 2006, p. 581)

8. I developed this argument more extensively and in more substantiated reference to Freud in the article on "Psychoanalysis" in *The Edinburgh Companion to Twentieth Century Philosophy* (Edinburgh University Press, 2007).

9. See, for example, *The Ethics of Psychoanalysis* (Lacan 1992), p. 314.

10. In this aspect of my inquiry, I have come close to a point made by Agnes Heller in her recently published impressive and thorough philosophical investigation of comedy. Heller situates comedy in relation to the zone

of the dovetailing between "two initial a prioris in human life": a social/cultural a priori and a genetic a priori. This is her basic argument:

> Since there is no initial connection between the two, and since only the experience of any single person can forge this connection, it is philosophically correct to speak about two a priories. . . . In the process of socialization those two a priories must come together; they must dovetail in order for the individual person even to survive. But—and this is my hypothesis—the two a priories cannot be entirely dovetailed; there remains a tension between them. To use another kind of metaphor, an unbridgeable abyss remains between the two a priories. I call this *existential tension* and an *existential abyss*. According to the conception of laughing and crying presented here, both of these are reactions to the impossibility of a real jump over the abyss; laughing and crying are responses to the failure of any complete dovetailing between the social and the genetic *a priori*. . . . While crying, one identifies oneself with the self of a fellow creature, feeling sorrow over the world's injustice, fate, and loss; whereas in laughing, one takes the position of the world, or of some idea about it, and laughs at the foolishness of people, one's own follies included. (Heller 2005, p. 201)

There are some similarities between this account and the one I am proposing here, but there are also some important differences, as should be clear from the discussion so far, as well as from the concluding remarks that follow.

BIBLIOGRAPHY

Aristophanes (1962). *The Complete Plays of Aristophanes.* New York: Bantam Books.

Aristotle (1982). *Aristotle's Poetics.* New York: Norton.

Badiou, Alain (1995). *Beckett. L'increvable désir.* Paris: Hachette.

Badiou, Alain (2006). *Logiques des mondes.* Paris: Seuil.

Benjamin, Walter (2004). "Fate and Character." In *Selected Writings,* ed. Marcus Bullock and Michael W. Jennings, vol. 1. Cambridge, MA: Harvard University Press.

Bergson, Henri (1999). *Laughter: An Essay on the Meaning of the Comic.* Copenhagen and Los Angeles: Green Integer Books.

Bloch, Olivier (2000). *Molière/Philosophie.* Paris: Albin Michel.

Canova, Marie-Claude (1993). *La comédie.* Paris: Hachette.

Cavell, Stanley (1981). *Pursuits of Happiness: The Hollywood Comedy of Remarriage.* Cambridge, MA: Harvard University Press.

Clemens, Justin, and Russell Grigg, eds. (2006). *Jacques Lacan and the Other Side of Psychoanalysis.* Durham: Duke University Press.

Critchley, Simon (2002). *On Humour.* London and New York: Routledge.

Deleuze, Gilles (1994). *Difference and Repetition.* New York: Columbia University Press.

Deleuze, Gilles, and Leopold von Sacher-Masoch (1991). *Masochism.* New York: Zone Books.

Descartes, René (1973). *Les passions de l'âme*, in *Œuvres philosophiques*. Tome III. Paris: Garnier Frères.

Descartes, René (1993). *Meditations on First Philosophy*. Indianapolis: Hackett.

Dolar, Mladen (1986). "Strel sredi koncerta." In Theodor W. Adorno, *Uvod v sociologijo glasbe*. Ljubljana: DZS.

Dolar, Mladen (2005a). "Comedy and Its Double." In *Schluss mit der Komödie! / Stop That Comedy!*, ed. Robert Pfaller. Vienna: Sonderzahl.

Dolar, Mladen (2005b). "Nothing Has Changed." In *Nothing/Nichts*, ed. Alenka Zupančič. Special issue of *Filozofski vestnik*, no. 2. Ljubljana.

Dolar, Mladen (2006). *A Voice and Nothing More*. Cambridge, MA: MIT Press.

Eco, Umberto (1992). *The Name of the Rose*. London: Vintage.

Freud, Sigmund (1969–1975). *Studienausgabe*. Frankfurt: Fischer.

Freud, Sigmund (1976). *Jokes and Their Relation to the Unconscious*. Harmondsworth: Penguin.

Freud, Sigmund (1977). *On Sexuality*. Harmondsworth: Penguin.

Freud, Sigmund (2001). *Papers on Metapsychology*. In *The Standard Edition of the Complete Psychological Works of Sigmund Freud*, ed. James Strachey, vol. 14. London: Vintage.

Gailus, Andreas (2006). *Passions of the Sign: Revolution and Language in Kant, Goethe and Kleist*. Baltimore: Johns Hopkins University Press.

Goldznik, Jean (1992). "Introduction." In Marivaux (1992).

Gouhier, Henri (1991). *Le théâtre et l'existence*. Paris: Vrin.

Hegel, G. W. F. (1977). *Phenomenology of Spirit*. Oxford: Oxford University Press.

Heller, Agnes (2005). *Immortal Comedy: The Comic Phenomenon in Art, Literature and Life*. Lanham: Lexington Books.

Hyppolite, Jean (1978). *Genèse et structure de la Phénoménologie de l'esprit de Hegel*. Paris: Aubier-Montaigne.

Janko, Richard (2002). *Aristotle on Comedy: Towards a Reconstruction of Poetics II*. London: Duckworth.

Kierkegaard, Søren (1983). *Fear and Trembling / Repetition*. Princeton: Princeton University Press.

Kleist, Heinrich von (1990). "Über die allmähliche Verfertigung der Gedanken beim Reden." In *Sämtliche Werke und Briefe. Vol. 3, Erzählungen. Anekdoten. Gedichte*. Frankfurt am Main: Deutscher Klassiker.

Lacan, Jacques (1986). *The Four Fundamental Concepts of Psycho-Analysis*. Harmondsworth: Penguin.

Lacan, Jacques (1988). *The Seminar of Jacques Lacan. Book II: The Ego in Freud's Theory and in the Technique of Psychoanalysis*. New York: Norton.

Lacan, Jacques (1991). *Le séminaire. Livre XVII. L'envers de la psychanalyse*. Paris: Seuil.

Lacan, Jacques (1992). *The Seminar of Jacques Lacan. Book VII: The Ethics of Psychoanalysis*. London: Routledge.

Lacan, Jacques (1994). *Le séminaire. Livre IV. La relation d'objet*. Paris: Seuil.

Lacan, Jacques (1998). *Le séminaire. Livre V. Les formations de l'inconscient*. Paris: Seuil.

Lacan, Jacques (2004). *Le séminaire. Livre X. L'angoisse*. Paris: Seuil.

Lacan, Jacques (2006). *Écrits*. New York: Norton.

Lacan, Jacques (2007). *The Seminar of Jacques Lacan. Book XVII: The Other Side of Psychoanalysis*. New York: Norton.

Laurent, Éric (2006). "Symptom and Discourse." In Clemens and Grigg (2006), pp. 229–253.

Legatt, Alexander, ed. (2002). *The Cambridge Companion to Shakespearean Comedy*. Cambridge: Cambridge University Press.

Marivaux (1992). *La fausse suivante. L'école des mères, La mère confidente*. Paris: Flammarion.

Marivaux (1993). *Le jeu de l'amour et du hazard*. Paris: Hachette.

Marx, Karl (1967). *The Eighteenth Brumaire of Louis Bonaparte*. Moscow: Progress Publishers.

Miller, Jacques-Alain (2006). "On Shame." In Clemens and Grigg (2006), pp. 1–28.

Molière (1971). *Œuvres complètes*. Paris: Gallimard.

Nietzsche, Friedrich (1978). *Thus spoke Zarathustra*. Harmondsworth: Penguin.

Pfaller, Robert (2006). "The Familiar Unknown, the Uncanny, the Comic." In *Lacan: The Silent Partners*, ed. Slavoj Žižek. London and New York: Verso.

Plato (1997). *Plato: Complete Works*, ed. John M. Cooper. Indianapolis: Hackett.

Plautus (1995). *Amphitryon*. In *Plautus: The Comedies*, ed. David R. Slavitt and Palmer Bovie, vol. 1. Baltimore: Johns Hopkins University Press.

Purdie, Susan (1993). *Comedy: The Mastery of Discourse*. New York: Harvester Wheatsheaf.

Regnault, François (1996). *La doctrine inoïe. Dix leçons sur le théâtre classique français.* Paris: Hatier.

Robinson, David (1989). *Chaplin: His Life and Art.* London: Paladin Books.

Santner, Eric L. (2006). *On Creaturely Life.* Chicago: University of Chicago Press.

Scott, Nathan A. (1965). "The Bias of Comedy and the Narrow Escape into Faith." In *Comedy: Meaning and Form,* ed. Robert W. Corrigan. San Francisco: Chandler Publishing.

Shakespeare, William (1986). *The Complete Works.* Hertfordshire: Omega Books.

Silk, M. S. (2002). *Aristophanes and the Definition of Comedy.* Oxford: Oxford University Press.

Simon, Alfred (1963). *Samuel Beckett.* Paris: Belfond.

Smith, Emma, ed. (2003). *Shakespeare's Comedies.* Malden, MA: Blackwell.

Sternberg-Grenier, Véronique, ed. (2003). *Le comique.* Paris: Flammarion.

Weininger, Otto (1993). *Spol in značaj.* Ljubljana: Analecta.

Žižek, Slavoj (1989). *The Sublime Object of Ideology.* London and New York: Verso.

Žižek, Slavoj (1999). *The Ticklish Subject.* London and New York: Verso.

Žižek, Slavoj (2004). *Organs without Bodies: On Deleuze and Consequences.* New York: Routledge.

Žižek, Slavoj (2006). *The Parallax View.* Cambridge, MA: MIT Press.

Zupančič, Alenka (2003). *The Shortest Shadow: Nietzsche's Philosophy of the Two.* Cambridge, MA: MIT Press.

Made in the USA
Middletown, DE
05 June 2023